Architecture isn't just for special occasions.

Expectations need to change.

Places for daily activities should be highly valued.

People can have more than they think.

We expect great qualities in buildings like museums;
shouldn't we also expect them in places for everyday living?

An individual's self-image is based on the quality of his or her daily life.

I want
my kids
to
feel safe.

I need
my
students
to have
freedom.

I want
a place
where I feel
welcome.

I like
a place
that'll never
change.

I want
a
great
nightcap.

I want to make a mess and not get in trouble.

Koning Eizenberg Architecture

Architecture isn't just for special occasions.

THE MONACELLI PRESS

Contents

Foreword

Making everyday places
has been an ongoing focus of this practice.
I have always been interested
in how mainstream culture and architecture intersect;
Hank Koning in how ideas are implemented;
and Brian Lane in how community benefit may be achieved.
Architecture is a collective effort,
and although the members of our team change over time,
they always seem to challenge expectations
and push our investigation further.

It has fallen to me as the cultural observer
to set down what has been learned.
Many clients and projects have been pivotal to our thinking,
influencing subsequent work.
We have drawn lessons
from all building types and budgets.
Fourteen of these projects are featured here.

—J.E.
Koning Eizenberg Architecture

Introduction

Over the last twenty years,
American cities have started to fill in.
Though this is not,
unfortunately,
a substitute for spreading out,
it does reflect an enthusiasm for urban living
and urban landmarks.
The potential of contemporary architecture
to contribute notable buildings
for special occasions,
such as museums, theaters, and city halls,
is highly valued.
At the same time,
the ability of architecture to enhance workaday urban living
is less well understood.
The buildings of daily life might, or might not,
be as declarative as those for special occasions,
but their role in the city is important nonetheless.

Most American cities
are works in progress,
and that is what is wonderful about them.
Inhabitation,
likewise, is a dynamic activity.
Buildings for programs of urban living,
from housing to work place to recreation center to school,
are inserted into an evolving context.
In our experience,
life is neither tidy
nor compartmentalized—
no matter how zoning regulations
attempt to systematize it
or aerial photographs
appear to order it.
Hauling the kids
from school to guitar lessons,
darting in for a forgotten aspirin,
juggling work and social commitments
mean that urban living is characterized
not by a sustained ceremonial experience
but by a myriad
of repeated
interlocking images, sounds, and smells.
These collected sensations
somehow stitch together
to form an urban setting.

Many of the fragments of urban living
are uplifting,
and many
are disappointing—
been to any nice drugstores lately?
In any event,
the organization and appearance of these parts
does not seem to give a picture comprehensive enough
to inform design decisions.
Like most, if not all architects,
we have undergone quite a bit of training
to distance ourselves
from conventions
of popular culture and everyday living.
At the same time,
we are asked to document and analyze a context
to justify why we should ignore it
or, conversely, why we should fit in.
Perhaps we are overly focused
on the physicality of a context
and need to take a closer look
at how life is actually lived within that context.
To do so means that we must trust what we experience
as much as what we learn.

Urban restructuring
that encourages mixed-use developments
(including affordable housing),
incorporates environmentally sustainable goals,
and expands public transportation
improves the framework of urban life.
Architecture is more specific,
taking a particular program and adding the delight
of nuanced space and form.
Architecture has the potential
to infuse social connection
and provide a simple joy of living
on a routine basis.

The role of architecture
in contemporary cities
can seem dwarfed by generic marketplace development
and low institutional expectations.
In these cases,
architecture is relegated
to ornamental trim or clever details.

On the other hand,
what energizes the American built environment
is simultaneously
the cocksureness of commerce and its ability—
or its failure—
to generate durable beauty.
It is essential
to recognize the business of development,
including the role of financing
and the practices of construction.
The building industry
is huge and risk averse, to be sure—
but knowledge enables change.
Understanding industry parameters
means they may be addressed effectively
and releases architecture to do more.
There are developers
and institutions
willing to invest in new ways of seeing and doing,
changing conventions by example.

It is not surprising
that the present tense is our preferred realm.
We like people.
We like it when people
get a kick out of architecture
or when they question design motives.
We like the ad hoc,
the discovered,
the legitimization of the unexpected.
We like it when owners and visitors
add their own mark:
people should feel welcomed,
not obliged.
The workaday context is full of opportunities
for deliberate acts of architecture.
Reframing expectations generates new prospects:
schools can provide rich environments
that celebrate living and learning,
not just places of instruction;
multiunit housing can be about the quality
of the experience of coming home,
not just about private space.
Making architecture for daily living
is a bit like making an indie movie.
Real life is a satisfying subject.

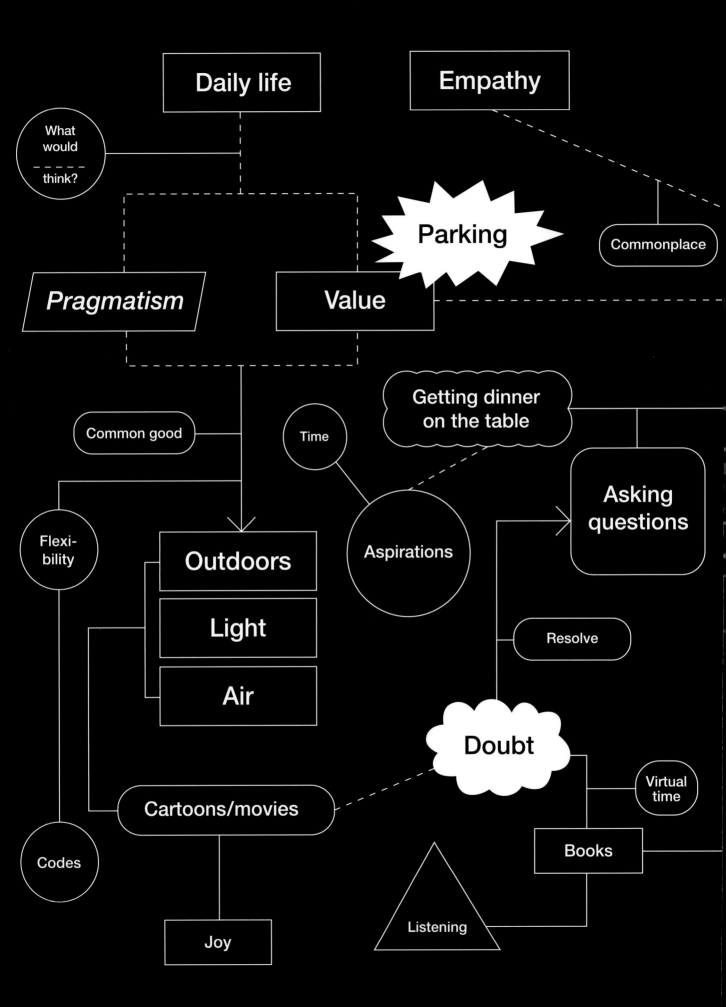

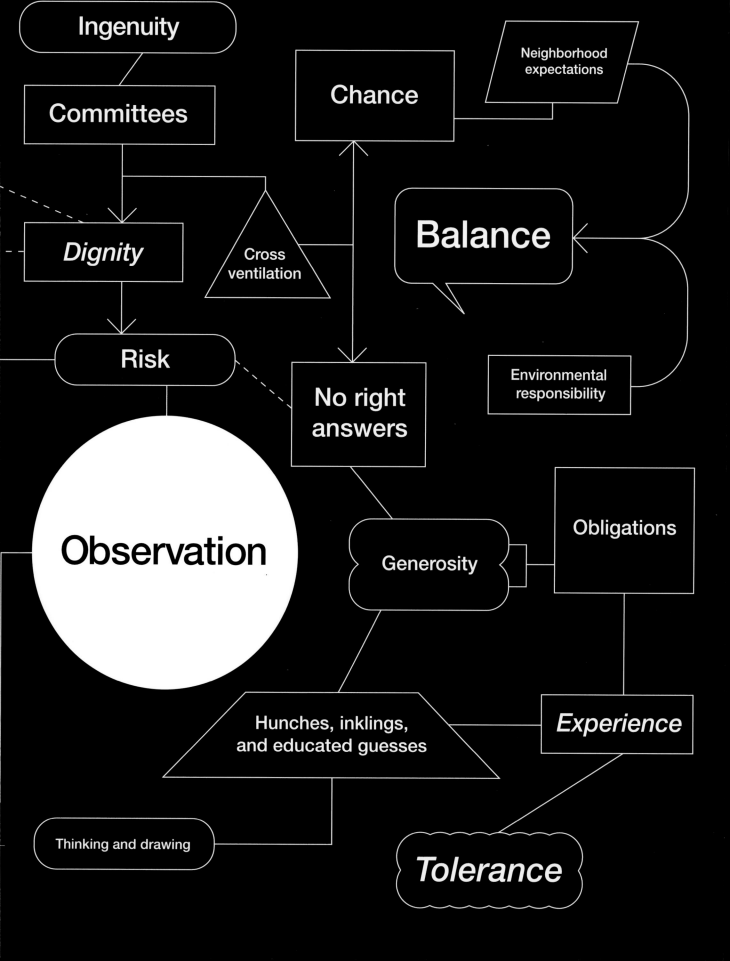

1.

Trust

There is a mismatch
between learned architectural preferences
and street experience, isn't there?
Many of my favorite spaces
are mocked in design circles;
nevertheless, I like strip malls and sentimental Victorian cottages.
Others are overlooked;
still, I am drawn to the layers of paint applied to cover graffiti
and, at the moment, the miniature landscape
growing under the curb of the storm-water drain
across the street.

I am not the only one who is trying to reconcile convention with observation.
Though the cool and messy quality of ordinary places
is often documented in architectural analysis,
it is rarely engaged.
Abstract form and complex spatial relationships
need not be at odds with an acknowledgment of the value and pleasure
of daily experience in a predominantly underdesigned world.

Because architects are entrusted with the making of place,
it also makes sense to calibrate architectural conventions
within the context of mainstream culture.
This means observing situations carefully
and trying to empathize with—
which is not to say conform with—
how others perceive value in architecture.
It helps to separate aesthetic preferences from practicalities
rather than to justify action by disguising one in the other.
Many clients—individuals, communities, cities—
do not trust architects because they cannot reconcile what we say with what we do.

There is untapped potential
in disengaging architecture from academia and the mainstream marketplace
(both highly conventionalized)
to set an experience-based evaluation of the built environment.
I do not see the value in universal truths—
a free form does not occupy higher moral ground
than a revivalist nineteenth-century porch.
Instead, it is the experience that counts—
how we make places rich in evocation;
how we translate dignity, sociability, community, and joy into architecture.
Trust is established not by convincing the world there is only one way
but by designing one to one.
I need eye contact to establish trust,
and I expect architecture to deliver the same.

West Hollywood Community Center

Plummer Park, in West Hollywood, extends north from Santa Monica Boulevard to Fountain Avenue. In 1998, the southern edge of the park was almost entirely obscured by a neglected parking lot and tired-looking community center—both of which were ours to improve. The park itself was a surprising discovery. Wedged between houses and apartment buildings, it felt more like a good friend's backyard than a conventional public place. On any day, it is a home away from home for seniors, many of them Russian émigrés; a smaller population of young families; teens; and a sizeable gay population. All of these constituencies participated in the community design process initiated by the city of West Hollywood to upgrade the community center. The initial idea was to rejuvenate the original building for seniors and to add a separate facility for teens.

Community processes are not about confrontation so long as they are structured well. In fact, they can be enjoyable and illuminating, as was the case at Plummer Park, where the interaction focused on mutual education about issues, parameters, and options. The process supported, rather than limited, design invention. A community committee was identified by the city to guide a series of evening meetings that were open to input from neighbors and the community at large. City staff assisted with input on programs and services. After a period of site analysis, the process moved forward to a reevaluation of the proposition of separate buildings for teens and seniors. We suggested a single intergenerational facility that would allow for more flexible programming and also address the community's interest in inclusivity.

The personality of the original community center was clearly not in line with the inviting and relaxed setting envisioned. With the budget so tight, it was not feasible to build all new, and we searched for seamless ways to integrate the old with the new. It was not even possible to significantly reconfigure the existing roof, a constraint that set in motion a strategy to disguise the rigid gables in a bigger gesture that also met conceptual expectations. The gables remain as one end of a single freeform folding canopy that extends some 320 feet to shelter the whole facility.

The design is a kind of scribble, loosely organizing courtyards, entries, and key spaces to set up a deliberate informality. At one end is the senior lounge (with fireplace and comfy chairs) and at the other the teen center (with game tables and homework room). In between are meeting and activity spaces. Outside, a new tree-canopied parking lot runs the length of the building. It was designed not only to bring a sense of the park to the street but also to acknowledge that people really *use* these places. Although often ignored, parking lots are real and important zones of activity. For buildings like community centers, they are key social spaces—as important as interior spaces—where people linger and continue conversations and encounters started indoors. In Australia, where I grew up, we call parking lots *carparks.* The moniker provides the right cue to rethinking parking lots as places of value.

Existing community center

A

B

C

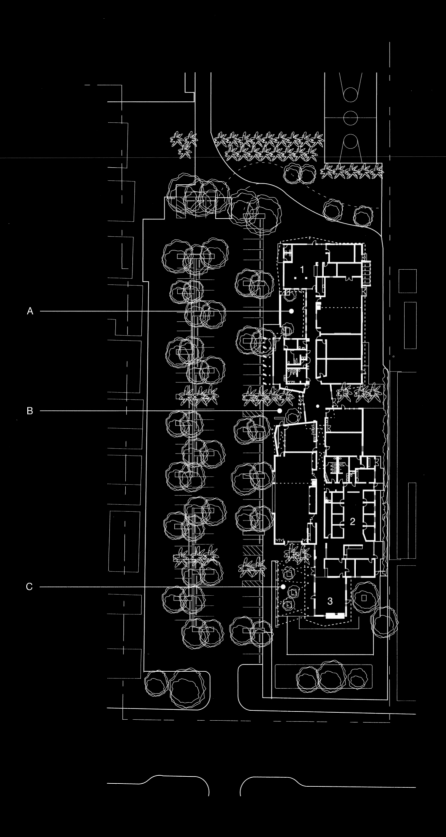

A

B

C

1 Teen lounge
2 Senior services
3 Senior lounge

N

Site Plan

0 8 16 32 Feet

↓ Park Office
← Teen Center
← Rooms 1-4
→ Rooms 5-6
→ Senior Lounge
→ Senior Activity Office
→ Social Services
→ Disability Services
→ Art Rooms 1-2
→ Computer Classroom
↔ Restrooms
EXIT

I'm able to meet new people here.

Ed Wolfe, 86

Masonry Variations Exhibit

Mike Menegazzi arrived at our office one afternoon with a book on Gaudí and a portfolio of tile and terrazzo projects. He had come to begin working on the design of a piece for the *Masonry Variations* exhibition to be held at the National Building Museum in 2003–4. The exhibition was sponsored by the International Union of Bricklayers and Allied Craftworkers and the International Masonry Institute. Mike and I were partnered by the curator, Stanley Tigerman, to design an installation that would push the limits of terrazzo. Other architect-craftworker teams were exploring brick, stone, and autoclave concrete. The project challenged both architect and craftworker to address the issue of making in the context of a rapidly changing construction industry.

A little background. Terrazzo originated on Roman building sites as a way to make use of waste marble. Over time, it has been formalized as a building material consisting of rounded marble chips (aggregate) set into a cement matrix or slurry. Once set, the rough surface is polished smooth. Traditional terrazzo is a half-inch or more thick; new plastic matrices, cheaper and easier to use, are less than one-quarter-inch thick. That the new application required less skill troubled Mike; however, the thinness of the new materials fascinated me. I started to wonder just how thin and even transparent terrazzo could be and, for that matter, what materials might be floated in the matrix—from glass to aluminum. Mike left to make some samples, and I pursued thin surfaces inspired by the rippling floors of ancient Herculaneum.

I had originally envisaged suspending thin, curved terrazzo panels from the ceiling and walls and backlighting them. Some panels were to be translucent; others would have glass aggregate. Terrazzo, however, is essentially a veneer and needs continuous support. Even if we reinforced the panels with fiberglass, we would be overstretching the material. I should have known better—mold-formed resin panels would have been a more appropriate way to achieve this particular effect. It was clear that designing for a particular material was very different from having an idea drive the choice of material—our normal methodology. Mike had also grown disenchanted. The application had stepped over the line for him. We had come to a not unfamiliar moment between craftworker and architect: Mike was holding onto traditions, and I wouldn't acknowledge any.

The next time around, I started thinking about how *little* needed to change to heighten the materiality of terrazzo. This approach resonated with Mike. A magazine image featuring a serpent made of jagged stone fragments fit our sense of frustration. It transmogrified by hand-drawn sketch into a kind of bearskin, starting on the wall and ending on the floor, made of shards of slate progressively more deeply embedded in cement. As the rug hit the floor, the slate was ground to achieve the polished appearance of terrazzo. There was no semblance of advanced technology. But this was a myth. The project would not have been possible without contemporary technology, particularly new adhesives and synthetic cement matrices. Equally deceptive was the apparent ease of fabrication. In fact, production took incredible skill.

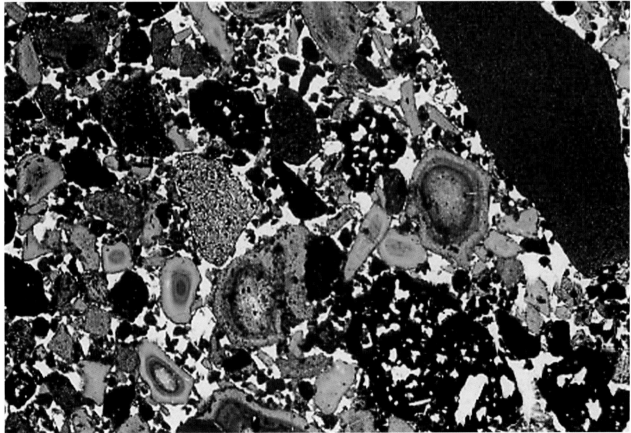

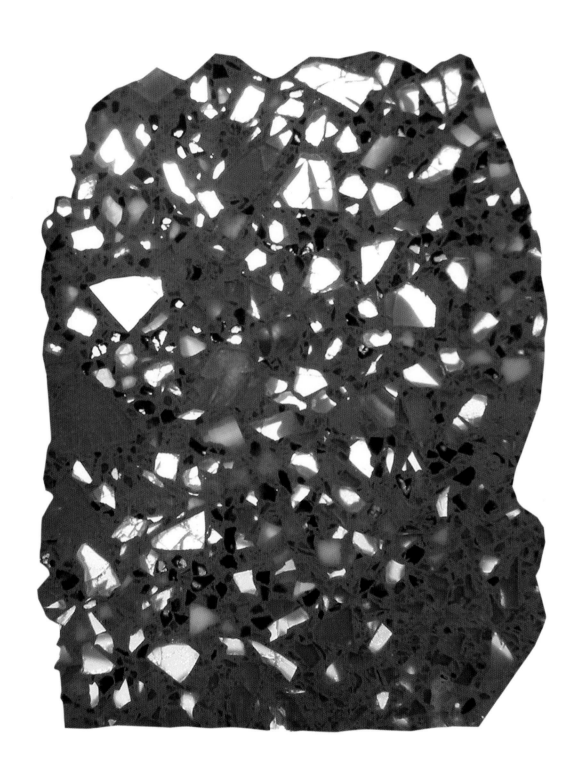

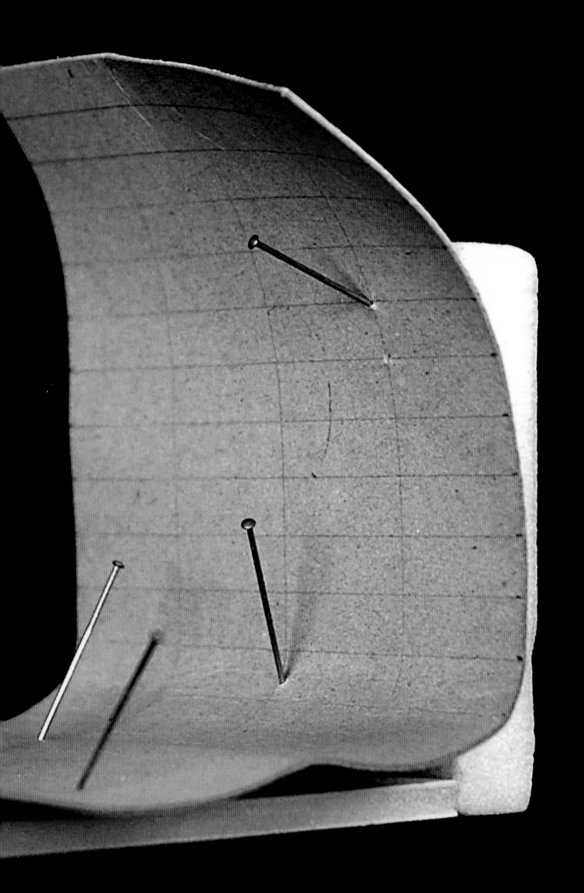

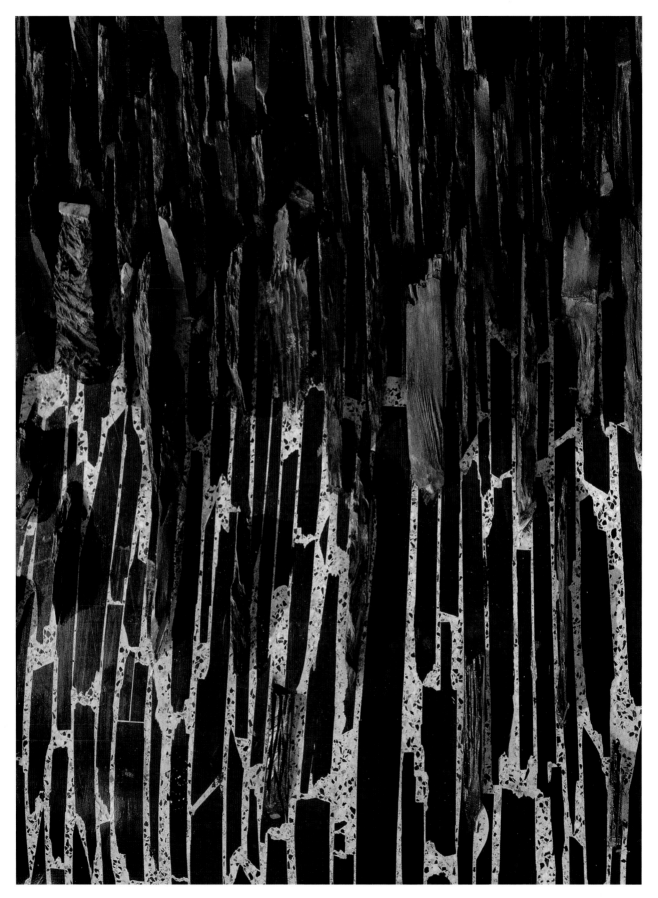

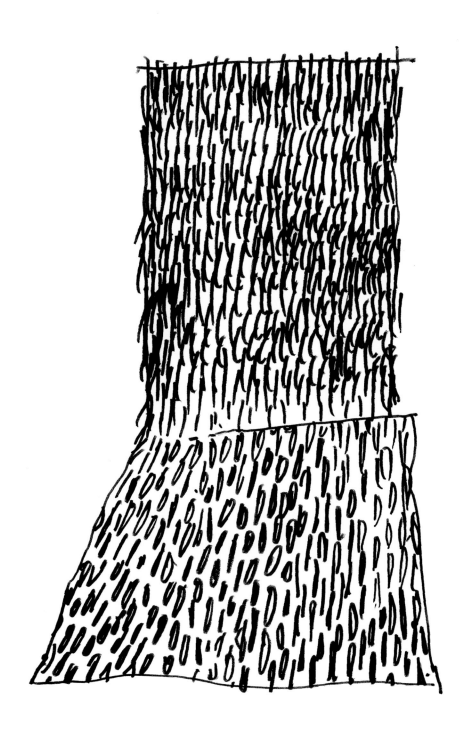

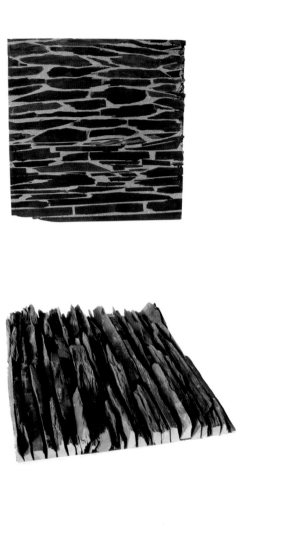
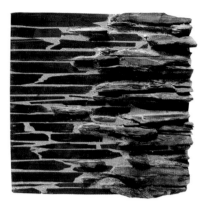

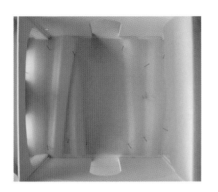

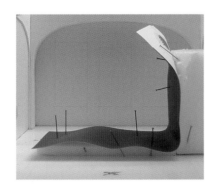
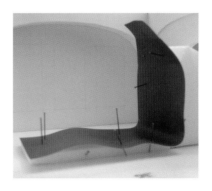

PS#1 Elementary School

FOR OUR LIBRARY, ELEMENTS THAT WOULD WORK —

- A LARGE SPACE THAT COULD BE DEFINED BY IT'S
PURPOSES — A STORY AREA, A MEDIA/REFERENCE AREA,
WORK AREAS WITH TABLES, LOW SHELVING, PILLOWS ᶜᴴᴵᴸᴰ ˢᴵᶻᴱᴰ
ACCESS TO LIBRARIAN, INFORMAL CHECK OUT SYSTEM, LON
LIBRARIAN + SOUND PROOFING, WALL SPACE FOR DISPLAYS
A PRIVATE AREA FOR LIBRARIAN + WORK AREA FOR PAREN?
STORAGE, SECURITY. ENOUGH ROOM FOR GROWTH OF COLLECT
FLEXIBILITY.

IT WOULD BE GREAT 'D HAVE IT ON THE FIRST FLOOR FOR EA
ACCESS FOR CHILDREN, PARENTS, AFTER + EARLY CARE ...

Lisa

May 21, 1996

Dear ___Abbie___

Thank you so much for joining us on our school site visits yesterday. I
hope that your time spent was as rewarding for you as mine was for me.
Sharing ideas in the abstract is valuable and helped us as we made a
program plan for our new campus; sharing ideas based on actual
experience in a school environment is even more valuable.

In order for us to benefit most from your participation on the site visits, it
would be helpful if you could write about the things that you liked and
didn't like that you saw at the different schools. Specifically I would
appreciate your listing at least three things that you liked at each campus
you saw and any new ideas that were generated by what you saw. Please
give me your writings in the next few days and I will pass them on to our
architects. Thanks.

JOEL

To refresh your memory, here is a list of schools (and Rec Center & home)
that we saw.

A.M.   P.M.

University Elementary School - Seeds   Wildwood
Berkeley Hall School Library   Rustic Canyon Rec Center
Curtis School   Koning/Eizenberg home
Village School

- UES
  - I liked the patio space, sliding doors opening up
    to patio
  - computers in classrooms for cooperative group work
    - large screen monitor for computer work/demo
  - library: small low tables with cushy pillows!
- Berkeley Hall
  1. entry way nook/counter - I liked the feeling. We'd need it
     to be on a smaller scale
  2. The story room had a good feeling
  3. Think about textures.

After Pluralistic School #1 in Santa Monica was completed in 1999, we were ceremoniously presented with 165 drawings and notes made by the students. The package came as quite a surprise. Some kids drew the roof trusses that pitched over their heads (there is a math lesson in the hyperbolic paraboloid roof). Others drew the front stairs and the concrete wall that supports them, noting the patterns of lugholes left by the formwork. A few children weren't interested in the architecture at all and drew the new computers instead. And other kids meticulously documented the assembly of the bridge that links the split campus high above an alley. That the bridge was a favorite place was not unexpected. In the predesign workshops, students favored exaggerated ways of moving around—they particularly liked ladders, bridges, and slides. In a learned world, a bridge across an alley is a liability; in an experiential world, it is a source of wonder.

All in all, the students noticed pattern, structure, color, and space. This is anecdotal evidence, to be sure, but it allowed us to trust our instinct that children are acute observers. Not every lesson about the world is extracted from guided instruction; kids absorb the knowledge and joy of living without direction—as do adults. This knowledge has affected every project we have designed since. Addressing function, economy, and durability fulfills only some of what is required in responsible learning environments. Schools, to be effective, must also support implicit learning with a rich architectural setting.

The adults at PS#1 are progressive educators and small-school advocates: they believe that school is about learning how to learn.

So it mattered to them that the kids could take control of their learning and by extension their environment. It was important, for example, that the students should be able to open a window and notice the breeze, or that classroom lessons on environmental responsibility should be reinforced by the sustainable design of the building itself. Other elements of the building may illustrate a lesson or may be discovered as a child connects received information with experience: the path of the sun as it is registered by the shadow pattern of the louvers, the math lesson embedded in the ceiling, the explicit expression of structure.

The design of a school environment can also collapse the artificial distinction between work and play. This distinction traditionally devalues the latter, yet in reality kids learn an enormous amount through play—how to share knowledge with their peers, how to exercise their imagination. Additionally, the distinction diminishes the pleasure to be found in work. Connecting interior (traditionally the domain of work) and exterior (the domain of play) is an important step in reuniting the two. At PS#1, all classrooms are naturally lit, with views to the outside and access to adjacent outdoor activity spaces.

Changes in school design are usually justified by bureaucratic statistics. For instance, since it has been shown that natural light increases test scores, school districts across the country have been encouraged to modify policies that preclude natural light in an effort to save energy use and/or prevent vandalism. I hope the 165 drawings by PS#1 students will also effect some change.

I enjoy the front yard and how you make a small space feel bigger than it really is. I really love how much more room we get in each room than on the east campus or the old part of the school.

— Jab Koning —

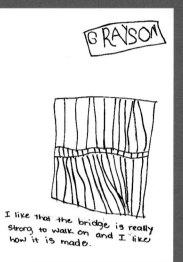

GRAYSON

I like that the bridge is really strong to walk on and I like how it is made.

Zig zags

JACK

This is the bridge. Under is my class.

AVERY

BROADWAY

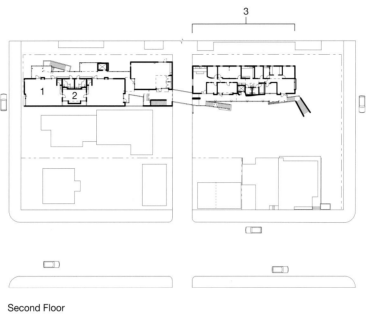

Second Floor

Twelfth Street

Alley

Euclid Street

Broadway

Ground Floor

1 Classroom
2 Workroom
3 Administration
4 Existing library
5 Existing multipurpose

N

0 16 32 64 Feet

I didn't know fresh air could inspire learning.

Nicole Dresch, 32, PS#1 Teacher

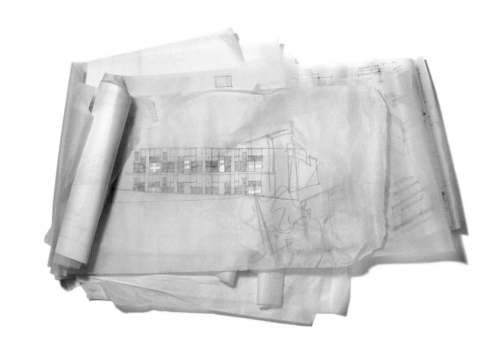

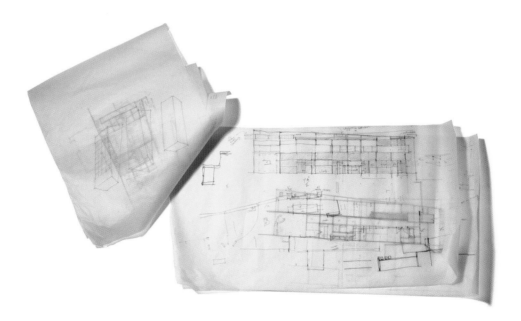

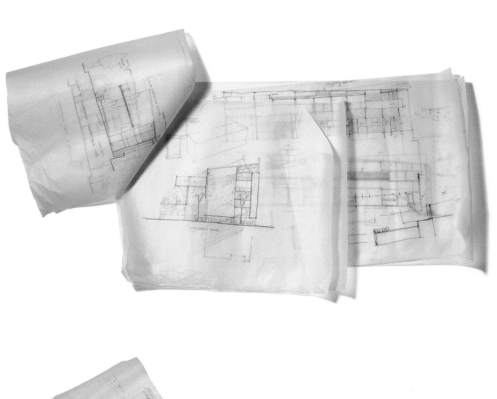

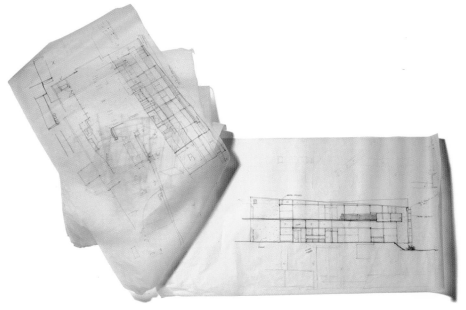

The Herb Alpert Educational Village

Nobody much trusts teens, but the New Visions Foundation does. Along with that refreshing point of view goes an enlightened idea about education—one based on trust, creativity, and community rather than on conformity and control. The foundation, led by Paul Cummins, sees great promise in looking at education as a community of interests centered on learning, a perspective that extends the potential of a school, its resources, and educational capacity. The New Roads School (currently on the Santa Monica site) will be the anchor of the campus, which will open in 2008. This independent school, which draws students from diverse backgrounds across the city, will be expanded to serve 675 students from kindergarten through twelfth grade. There will also be a preschool for 75 children, programs for children with disabilities, and space for Mommy & Me classes. More unusually, an area of 7,500 square feet is set aside for nonprofit organizations, including the foundation, that develop and/or outsource programs for children. The foundation intends to host educators at seminars and conferences and will also make the campus available as a community resource. It is not surprising that the concept of a village appealed to New Visions—it implied safety, shared interests, community support, and social responsibility. While the typical village is nestled in rolling green hills, our site is located amid production studios and asphalt—well, if the foundation could trust teens, we could make sense of the context.

The educators asked for the expected (or at least what should be expected): a sustainable design with daylit, naturally ventilated classrooms and amenities like a library and a gym. They also asked for the less expected, encouraging us to think about informal opportunities for student/staff interaction. One outcome that emerged from this process was the *newsroom:* the library's periodicals section doubles as reception for the academic offices. The creative arts are fundamental to the curriculum; to this end, spaces are dedicated to art, film, and movement. Plans also include a performance space designed specifically for orchestral music that can be configured for drama and dance. Such a finely tuned performance space might seem extravagant for a school—but the foundation approaches education differently, seeing in the investment validation of the program as well as a recognition of the worth of children and young adults.

Certain aspects of the village ideal will always hold sway— the sylvan setting that instills a sense of peace and safety, the idiosyncratic layout that encourages exploration. Frustrated by the gritty surroundings but encouraged by the educators' commitment to natural beauty, we turned the idea of a village inside out. The buildings are pushed to the perimeter of the site and wrap around a sequence of green spaces akin to a walled Chinese garden. As in a village, circulation is organized so that choices made are never wrong. Paths lead past windows and activities to offer opportunities for pausing and interaction, crossing big spaces that anticipate community events. There is always more than one route, and there is always something to see. The setup supports both amble and efficient walk. The benefit is measured in expanding potential rather than saving time.

Theater

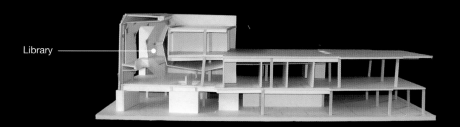

Library

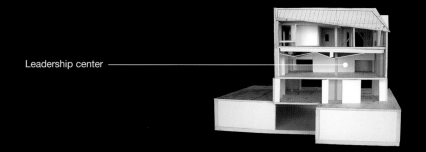

Leadership center

Elementary school
and preschool

Performance hall

Leadership center
and not-for-profit

Library

Gym

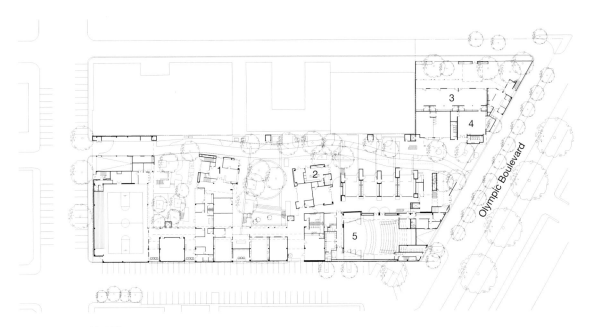

First Floor

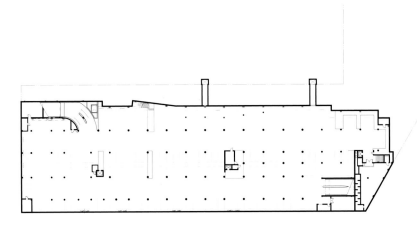

Basement

1 Academic offices
2 Café
3 Preschool
4 Elementary school
5 Performance space

6 Library
7 Leadership center
8 Non-profit offices

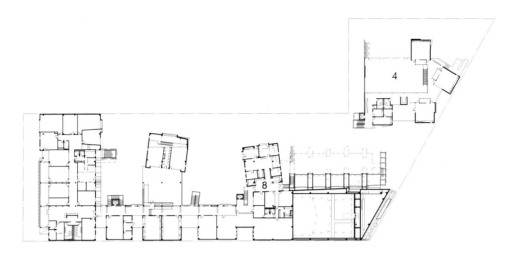

Third Floor

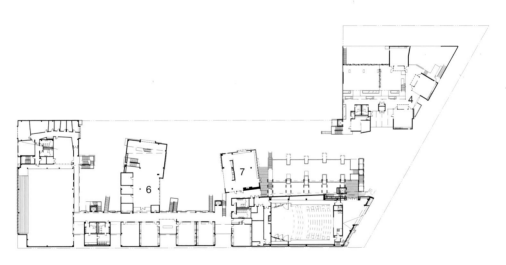

Second Floor

N

0 32 64   128 Feet

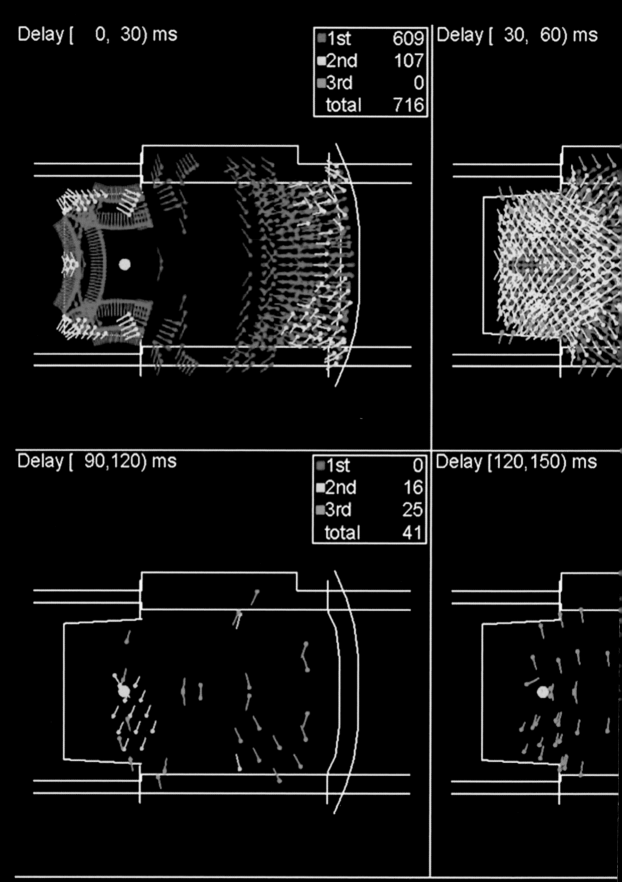

Delay [0, 30) ms

■1st	609	
■2nd	107	
■3rd	0	
total	716	

Delay [30, 60) ms

Delay [90,120) ms

■1st	0	
■2nd	16	
■3rd	25	
total	41	

Delay [120,150) ms

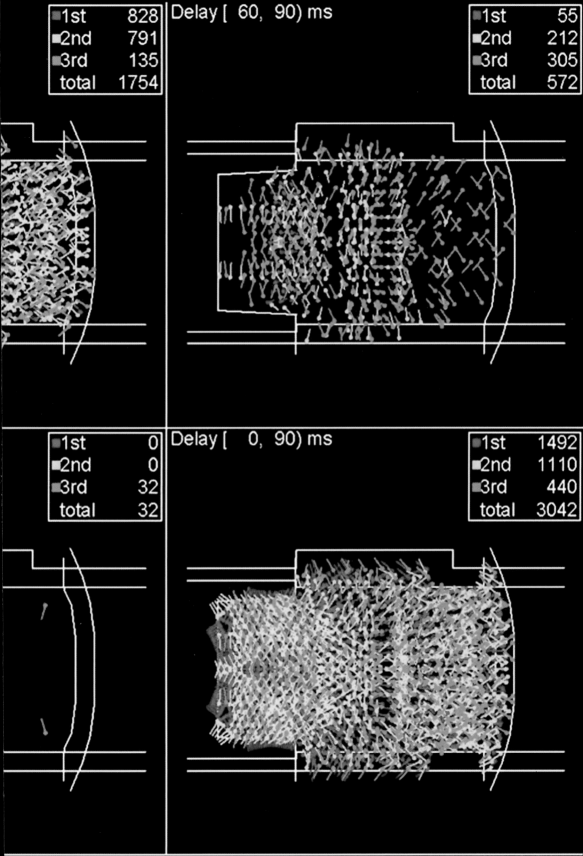

Delay [60, 90) ms

1st	828
2nd	791
3rd	135
total	1754

1st	55
2nd	212
3rd	305
total	572

Delay [0, 90) ms

1st	0
2nd	0
3rd	32
total	32

1st	1492
2nd	1110
3rd	440
total	3042

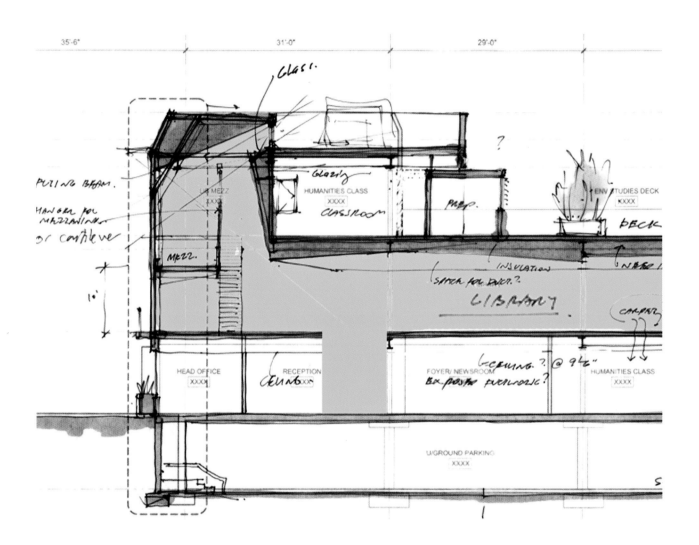

35'-6"   31'-0"   29'-0"

GLASS.

PURLIN BEAM.

HANGER FOR MEZZANINE

or cantileve

Glazing

HUMANITIES CLASS
XXXX

CLASSROOM

LIB MEZZ
XXXX

MEZZ.

PREP.

?

INSULATION

SPACE FOR DUCT.?

LIBRARY

10'

HEAD OFFICE
XXXX

RECEPTION
CEILING XXX

FOYER/ NEWSROOM
Exposed structure?

U/GROUND PARKING
XXXX

CEILING ? @ 9'6"

ENV STUDIES DECK
XXXX

DECK

NEED

CARPET

HUMANITIES CLASS
XXXX

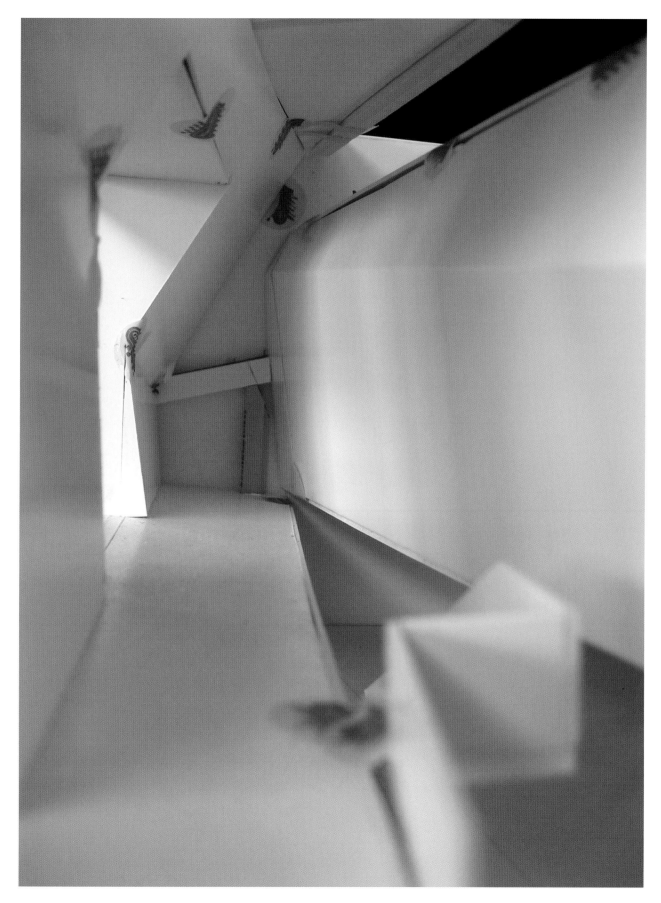

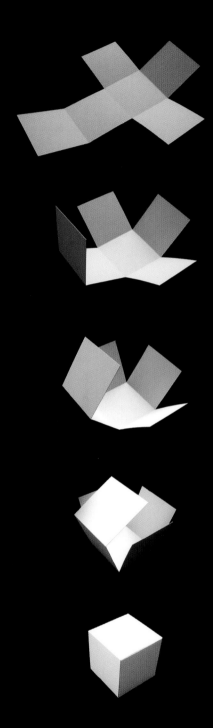

Harold Way Apartments

When you design a place for families to live, what are the responsibilities? What if the place is an apartment building of fifty or so affordable units (eighty-one dwelling units per acre) in Hollywood, California? The developer (a dedicated not-for-profit), which must compete for funding, rightfully demands economy, which means you have to do all the usual things: plan sensibly, align like units, avoid structural gymnastics, cross ventilate to avoid air conditioning, and more. But you also have to ask what is important for everyday living. These days, safety and cleanliness go without saying. But then there are the little things (and the big things) that make it nice to get up in the morning, come home at night, and hang around on the weekend. You can try to make life sweeter by planting trees at the end of a vista, organizing a big courtyard for kids to play, and locating a laundry and barbeques as social hubs, but you can't count on any particular outcome. In practice, each family and each community works out how a place will actually be used. As architects, it can be a little frustrating—perhaps it is best thought of as a kind of cinema verité where architects facilitate rather than control the action.

Another type of responsibility is the communication of those things in the art of architecture you care about most. This is part of an implied agreement with any user of a building as well as with the community at large. We get great pleasure from inventive compositional organization, from rhythm and sequence heightened by the ornament of shadow, color, and texture. In affordable housing, this strategy is executed under the tightest of parameters—on a pure design level, it is intensely interesting, a sort of Su Doku puzzle. At the Harold, for example, completed in 2003, the thin center building zigzags and is clad in cement board and wood battens (a nod to comforting traditional siding), which will one day be grown over by flowering vines. The costs of the stretched envelope (more exterior wall) and the more expensive cladding are offset by a spare and very efficient approach for the two flanking stucco-clad buildings. The zigzag and the cement board/wood combination add variety of shape, evocation, and material and also define the large courtyard in a casual way. I can see that the kids set up Barbies, magic ponies, and dollhouse paraphernalia in the laundry and in the courtyard; I have to trust that a formal design move is worthwhile as well.

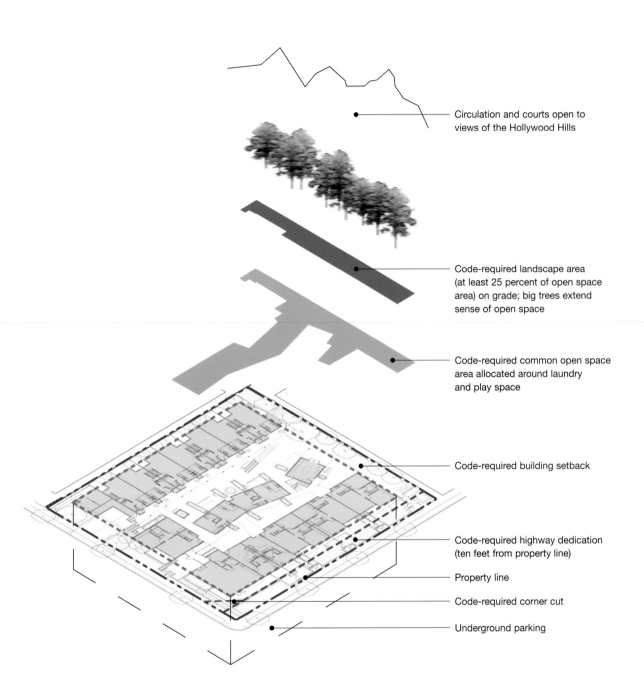

Circulation and courts open to views of the Hollywood Hills

Code-required landscape area (at least 25 percent of open space area) on grade; big trees extend sense of open space

Code-required common open space area allocated around laundry and play space

Code-required building setback

Code-required highway dedication (ten feet from property line)

Property line

Code-required corner cut

Underground parking

Two-bedroom flats

One-bedroom flats

Patio

Subterranean parking

Entry court

Three-bedroom townhouses

Elevator   Major court   Patio

Western Avenue

Harold Way

1 Entry
2 Community room
3 Mail
4 Laundry
5 Barbecues
6 Play area

N

0   8   16   32   Feet

This is a better place for my family.

Adam Gonzalez, 38, Harold Way resident

Ease

For us, architecture is personal—
one person making something for another.
We like comfortable relaxed spaces
that allow us to feel in control,
so that is the kind of place we want to make for others.
Strong visual and physical connections between inside and outside
support an intuitive sense of freedom.
Outdoors, informality is natural
and expectations of social behavior are less inhibited—
something as simple as spilling a drink does not invoke the usual consequence.
Is it possible to capture that sensibility in built space?
In both intent and production,
it seems to require generous gestures
and the appearance of effortlessness.
Design has to look easy to feel easy.

Generating ease,
particularly in low-budget projects,
involves getting the better of a construction process
that has become more bureaucratic than effective.
Buying more for less
requires intense examination of the practicalities.
That undertaking is more enjoyable than many might think.
In our practice, it translates into a kind of superpragmatism
that underlies each of our projects—
knowing the codes well enough to take advantage of them;
extracting design opportunity
from a construction or programmatic constraint.
All the while, we have to wonder
at the irony of current planning and building codes
that are so anachronistic that making things look easy
requires extraordinary effort.

More often than not,
we don't meet the people who occupy
or interact with what we make.
So in our heads, we *inhabit* each project as we design.
We walk through every building,
come home to every house,
sit at every desk for the first time or the fiftieth time,
and ask ourselves, over and over, is it worth it?
Do we feel welcome here,
would we hang out, is there more to discover?
When a project is complete,
it is for others to interpret.
Architecture doesn't come with an instruction manual.

25th Street Studio

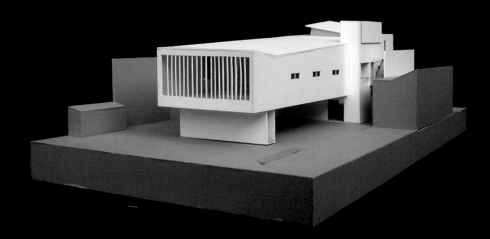

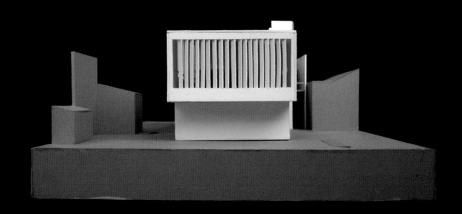

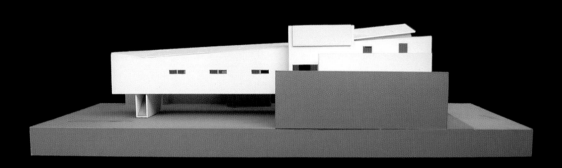

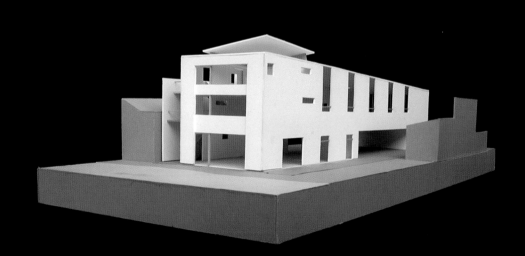

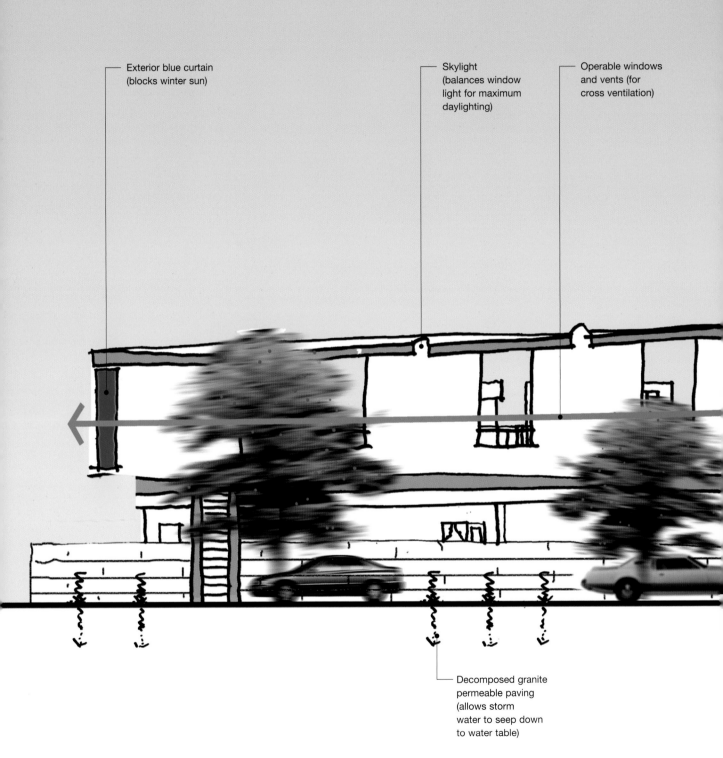

Exterior blue curtain
(blocks winter sun)

Skylight
(balances window
light for maximum
daylighting)

Operable windows
and vents (for
cross ventilation)

Decomposed granite
permeable paving
(allows storm
water to seep down
to water table)

162

Photovoltaic panels

Street tree
(shades
morning sun)

People, like us, who love the act of building have their own sense of logic. That logic is instrumental to conceptualizing a project. Function is a paradigm, and challenging the code when it seems bureaucratic (so much of the time) is a sport. Builders also get a thrill out of tinkering and speed. So as we thought about how to develop a small infill site in Santa Monica (a studio for ourselves as well as some rental space), we did what we always try to do— strip away as many constraints and complexities as possible to extract commonsense parameters. The 5,600-square-foot project was built over nine months in 1999 for $520,000. That felt good.

Common sense may seem too simplistic a strategy to provoke formal consequence, but it is not. It underpins our efforts to generate ease, economy, and unpretentiousness. For us, common sense is not about habit; it is an approach that capitalizes on the pragmatic and on generally accepted knowns. In this case, it was more what we *didn't* do that produced the personality and form of the building. We avoided subterranean parking—it would have been too expensive and time-consuming. We minimized construction at the site boundary so that there would be limited need for expensive fire-rated walls. Unexpectedly, the resulting project more closely resembled the neighboring lazy dingbat apartments of the 1950s than contemporary development—a coincidence that appealed to us.

This is not to say that we didn't have arguments about shape and space. There are always hundreds of ways to shape and squeeze the design in terms of its proportion, disposition, materials, and sense of volume. Design has a kind of built-in loop. While commonsense principles may set the concept, evolving compositional choices test the power of that concept. Ideas may be scrapped or retained based on how their opportunities play out.

Even with an eye to practicality and economy, we ran short of money and had to delay the incorporation of passive shading and other sustainable strategies. In the last few years, we have added photovoltaics on the roof, movable translucent Polygal louvers on the northwest (hooked up to a garage-door opener), and a big blue exterior curtain, which evolved from an improvised blue tarpaulin sunshade, on the southwest. The blue shade is now a permanent fixture that casts watery light on winter afternoons.

West Street Community Center

One year after the World Trade Center tragedy, the *New York Times Magazine* published a special issue that included a proposal for Manhattan. The exploratory proposition was spearheaded by Herbert Muschamp to suggest opportunities for a devastated community. The plan was generated by the idea of reuniting Lower Manhattan by burying West Street and reinstating the street grid. Various architects were asked to propose housing, offices/retail, hotels, and a library; we contributed a vision for a community center.

Rebuilding community starts with program, and the program we were given included recreation facilities with room for teens and younger kids; neighborhood retail (previously missing from the area), including big bookstore, cafés, and a farmers market; winter garden; community conference center; senior center; and senior housing. Even though the design was a visualization, and not a real scheme, we took the project very seriously, down to the fire exits.

It was hard to keep fact and fiction separate, or to find a way to make sense of loss. In the end, we drew on what we knew we could convey with honesty—personal memories of New York. It was the more casual interactions that came to mind: clothes shopping and a fabric exhibit at the Museum of Modern Art were conflated into the west-facing pleated awning; the recollection of an old recreation center in Brighton Beach, Brooklyn (seen while visiting relatives), inspired the coloring.

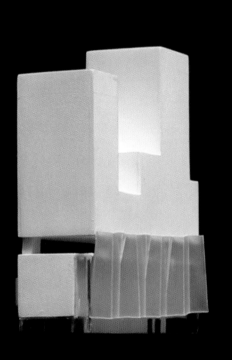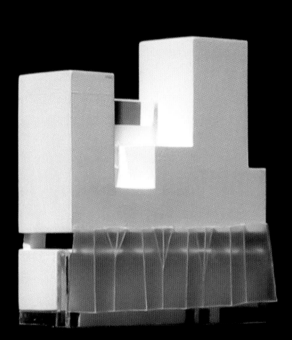

Site for community center

SENIORS

CONFERENCE

SERVICES

POOLS

GYMS

TEENS

KIDS

The Standard Downtown L.A.

In the old black-and-white episodes of "Perry Mason," set in Los Angeles, the Superior Oil Building appears in the opening credits—it is Perry's office. The continuity problems are hard to miss: the terrace that appears to open off the office couldn't possibly belong to the same building. We ran into continuity problems of our own in 2000 as we converted the headquarters for the Superior Oil Company into a hotel.

The historic building, designed by Claude Beelman in 1956, fronted on Flower Street. But it was impossible to accommodate the pick-up and drop-off needs of a modern hotel in the same location. So we reversed the entry sequence, reinventing the back of the building as the front; now a new entry courtyard leads to a new front door cut into a concrete wall.

The Standard hotels, owned by André Balazs, target young, party-loving travelers on a budget. The downtown Standard's aesthetic, developed with interior designer Shawn Hausman, was early 1960s, and although the exterior of the building had the right look, the public spaces—save the historic elevator lobby at the old front door—all dated from the 1980s or later. The sequence of public spaces exploited the constraints of structure, code, and budget to contrast exaggeratedly intimate spaces (like the new coffee shop) with grand-scaled spaces (like the big lobby) and reframe leftover features (like the escalators) as clever accessories. The upper floors were gutted and guest rooms configured to make sense of the oversized office floor plates. Most guest rooms have glass-walled bathrooms to draw daylight and a sense of space from the room itself.

The incredible popularity of the rooftop pool and bar was not entirely a surprise. The bar inhabits what was once the marble-clad mechanical space, and a new raised roof deck accommodates the pool. While pools and bars are both traditional social attractors, even more is at play here: the appeal is enhanced by the intrigue of the journey. The rooftop is not so easy to find—the lobby escalator rises to a mezzanine, where a hallway leads to the one small elevator to the roof. As the elevator opens, the dizzying geography of the destination— twelve floors up and encircled by office towers—is exhilarating. Conventional wisdom would say that the end result would not offset the difficulty of the journey, but conventional wisdom does not value highly enough (or even recognize) either the joy of discovery or the buzz of the unexpected.

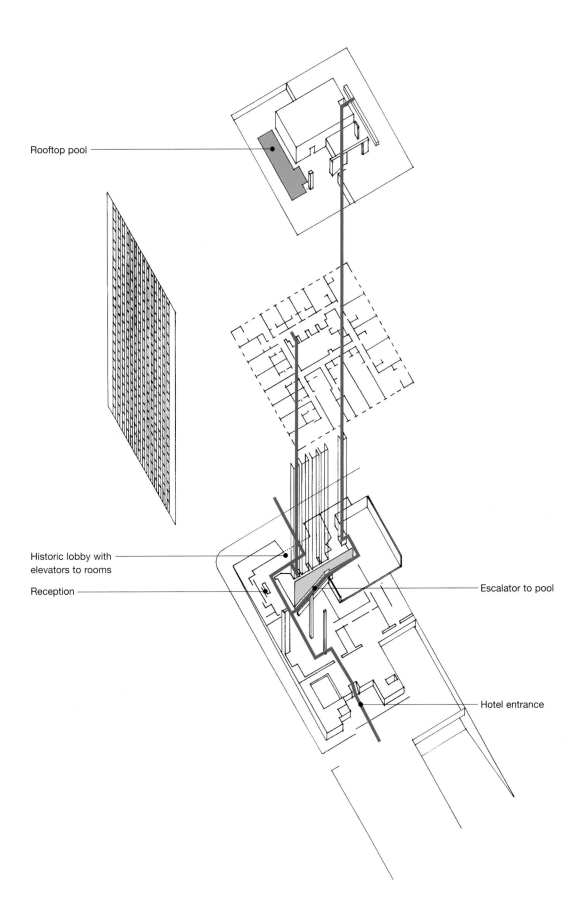

Rooftop pool

Historic lobby with
elevators to rooms

Reception

Escalator to pool

Hotel entrance

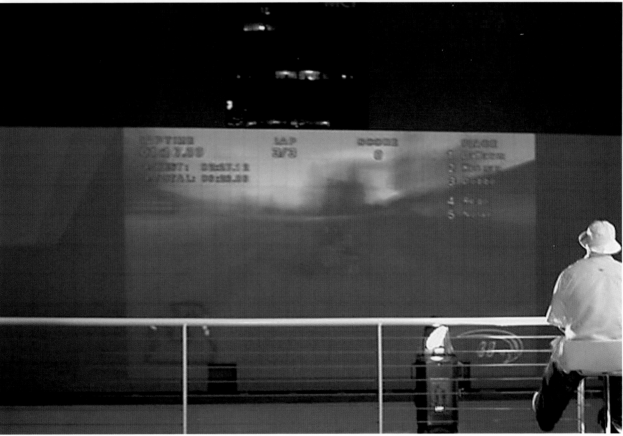

I didn't expect a roof with a pool and vibrating waterpods.

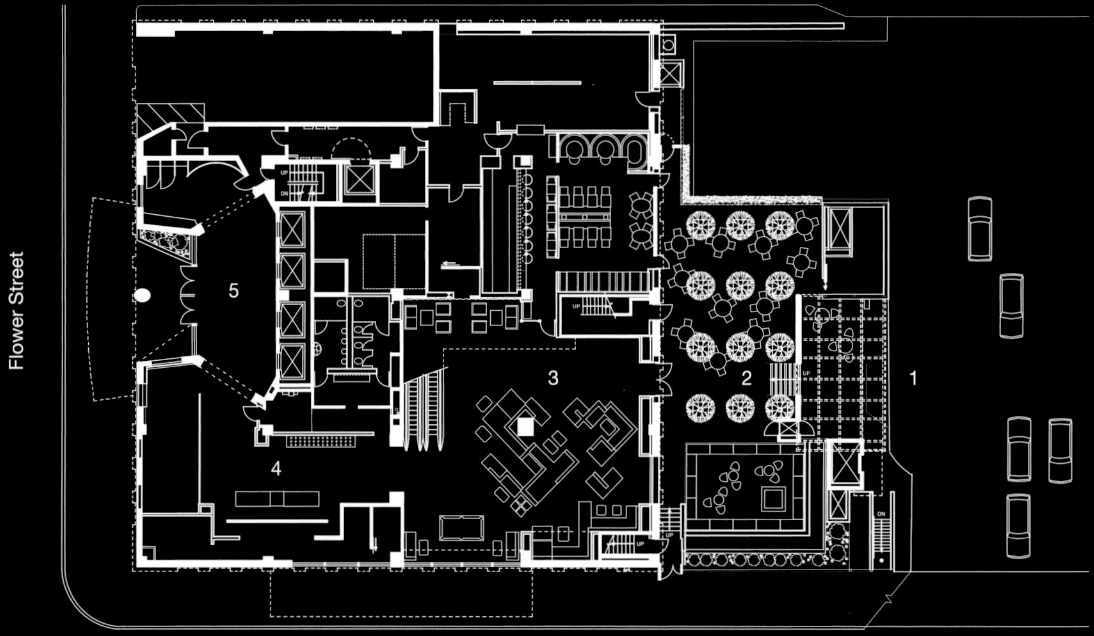

Flower Street

Ground Floor

Sixth Street

1 Drop-off
2 Courtyard
3 Lounge
4 Reception
5 Historic lobby

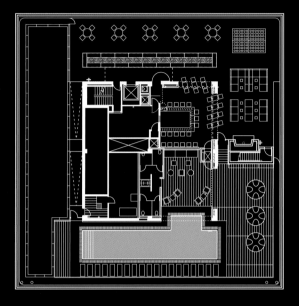

Roof Level

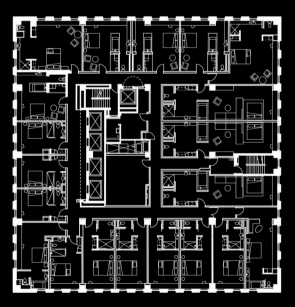

Typical Guestroom Level

N

0   8   16   32   Feet

Hancock Avenue Housing

The mixed-use development on Hancock Avenue in West Hollywood will provide tick-the-box city living. The location is just right, with a coffee- and newsstand on the corner, a planned restaurant, nearby bus stops, a weekend street scene, and a quiet neighborhood to the north. A series of community meetings held in 2002 set the mix of four floors of housing (38 units), retail space (10,000 square feet), and public and residential parking (207 spaces). Visualizing the design as a cable knit best approximates how the odd-shaped, sloping lot and the building program were combined into a coherent whole. The section is the key: the need to separate public and private parking while insisting on street-friendly housing along Hancock pushed residential parking up and over that housing, to the third level, where the parking area expands the rooftop landscape.

Multiunit housing is an aggregation of small pieces; these never seem to coalesce without secondary, smaller-scale moves—the ones that push and pull on the big idea. These moves are not always set with the initial concept. In this case, due to delays with the entitlement process, the design was not fleshed out until a few years later. The secondary moves included development of the sliding exterior sunscreens on the south-facing flats, the proportion of outdoor rooms on the Hancock-facing garden units, and the seemingly casual distribution of the cabana units, which accumulate to present a kind of hillside appearance from the west.

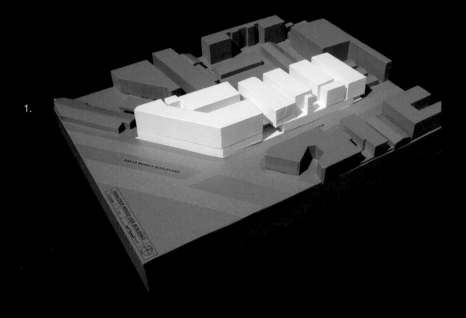

1.

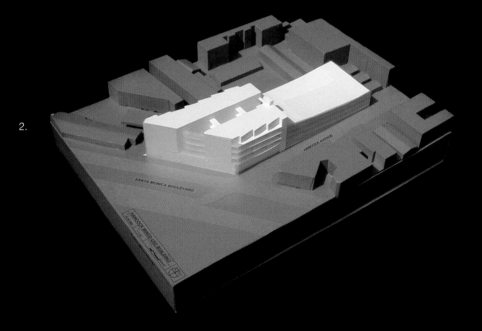

2.

Community Process Models

1 Maximum number of housing units
2 Maximum number of parking spaces
3 Hybrid
4 As approved (four floors only)

3.

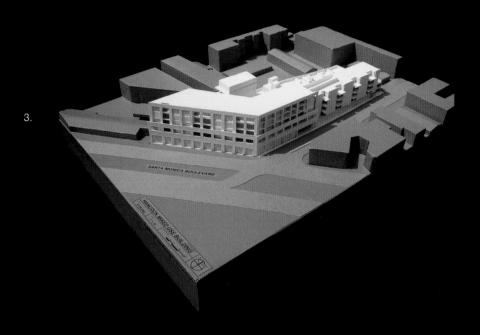

4.

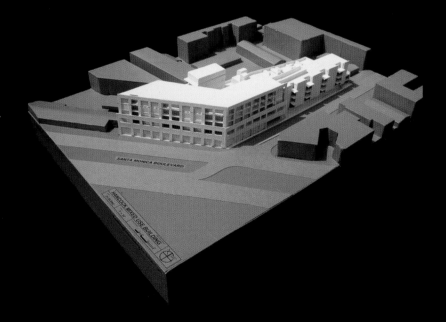

Second Floor

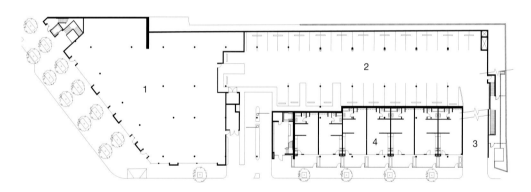

Ground Floor

1 Retail
2 Public parking
3 Up to residential parking
4 Rental units
5 Cabana units
6 Residential parking
7 Flats
8 Garden units
9 Arbor

Fourth Floor

Third Floor

N   0   25   50   100   Feet

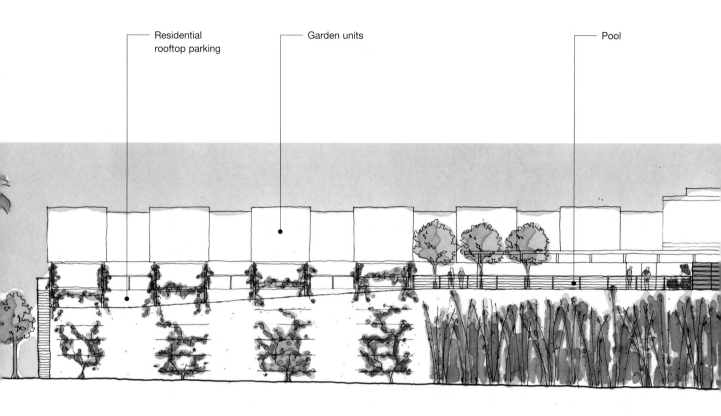

Residential rooftop parking   Garden units   Pool

Santa Monica Boulevard   Hancock Avenue   Flats

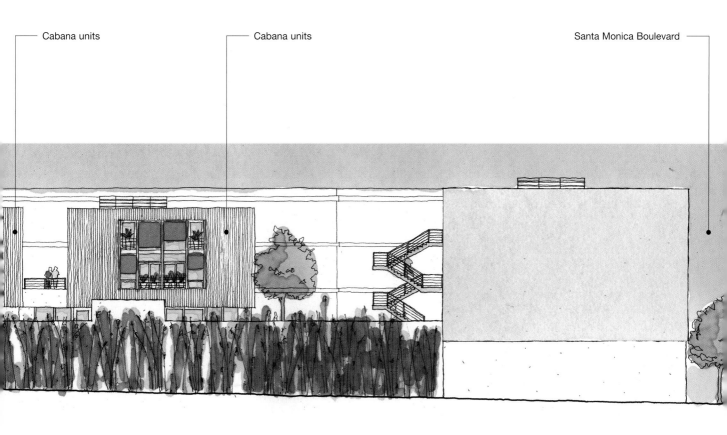

Cabana units Cabana units Santa Monica Boulevard

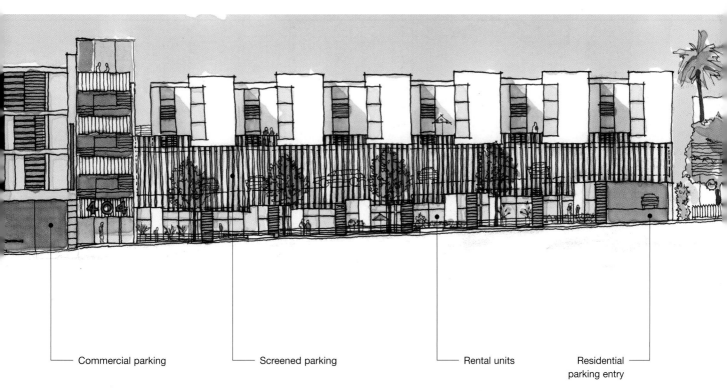

Commercial parking Screened parking Rental units Residential parking entry

233

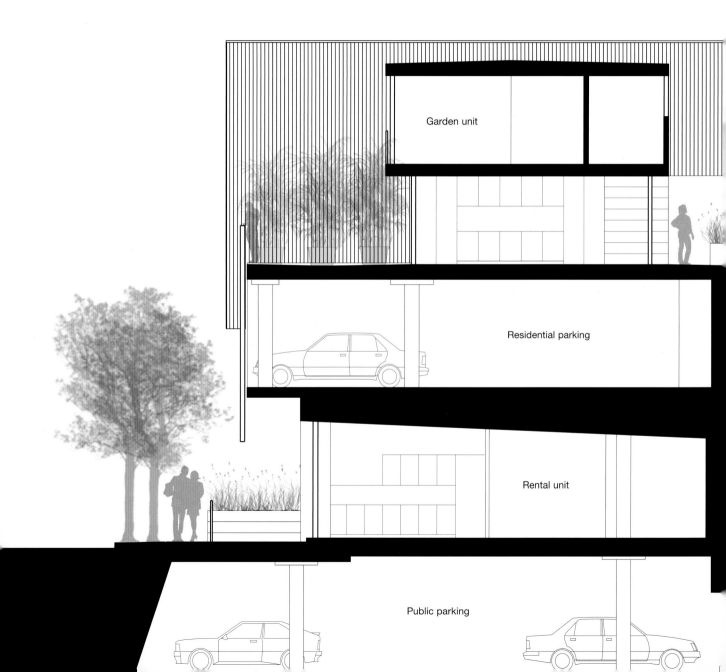

Garden unit

Residential parking

Rental unit

Public parking

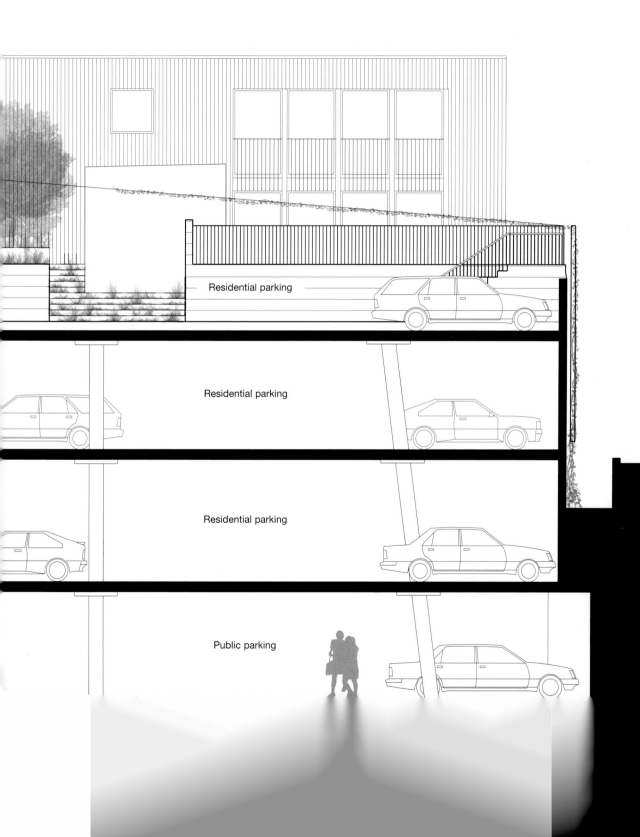

Residential parking

Residential parking

Residential parking

Public parking

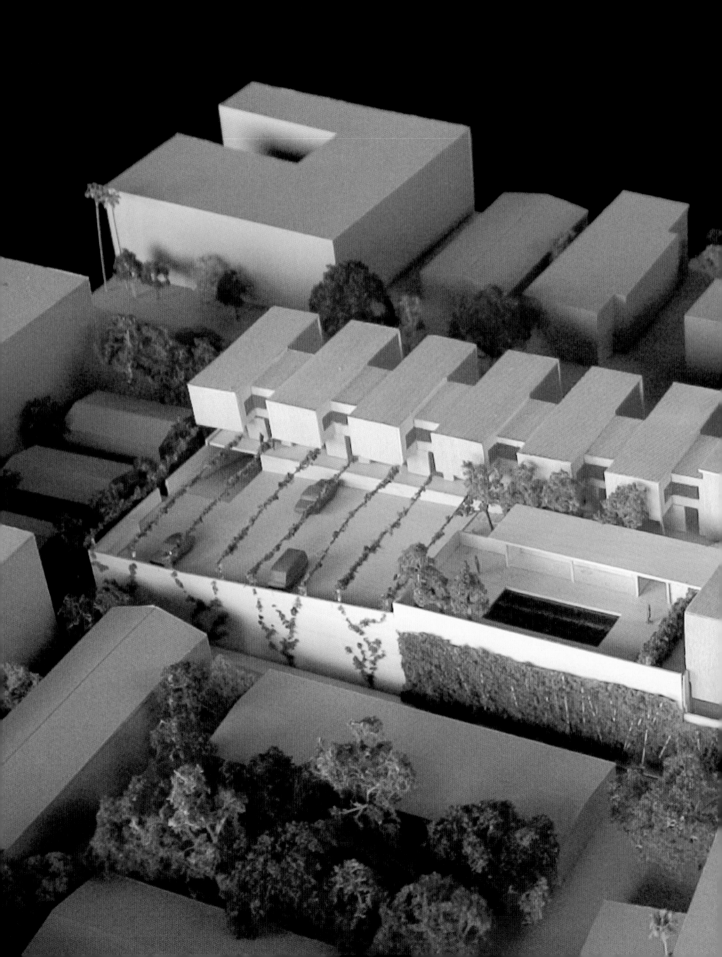

11th Street House

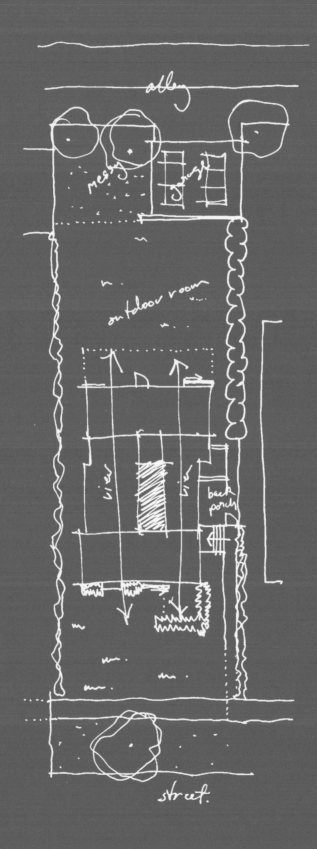

The typical real-estate advertisement runs like this: "3bed, 3bath, den, great indoor/outdoor connections. Suits young family." We know lots of families who would like a house like this— one of them was the Shines. They had bought a quarter-acre lot with a little old house in Santa Monica, and they wanted a bigger modern house. In real-estate terms, "modern" is a catchall for anything that cannot be called Cape Cod, Mediterranean, or traditional. The term is not used very precisely but usually applies to houses where details rather than ornament prevail, where the plan is open and light, and where large areas of glass are featured.

By Los Angeles standards, the Shines didn't want a large house, and they didn't want an expensive house—that is, they were hoping to build their dream home of about 2,900 square feet for about $160 per square foot. That was cheap in urban Los Angeles, even in the late 1990s. It's hard to believe that building cheap modern houses in sunny California would be difficult— the midcentury Case Study houses seemed to have solved that problem long ago. But no. Those pretty, thin-roofed, glass-expansed prototypes are no longer so cheap. This is due in part to contemporary seismic and energy codes, which have increased the hidden costs of structure and glazing.

In fact, these expenses have made building this kind of house relatively costly. Some architects are investigating prefabrication— as architects did in the 1950s—in an effort to address increasing expenses. In this case, we were more interested in how to minimize costs of on-site construction, using tried-and-true wood shear walls and avoiding expensive steel and custom framing connections. This meant providing a certain amount (about eight feet) of continuous, full-height solid wall on each building face, which in turn decreased the glass area, further reducing cost. The trick was to infuse this expedient strategy with design intent—on the east facade, for example, the wood and glass are grouped to act as one.

The original proposal had been to remodel the existing house. By the time it became clear that none of it was worth saving, the plan had been established, and we realized that the simple vernacular setup with its standard ceiling heights and simple form provided a good cheap backdrop for a few relatively expensive, focused interventions. These features—the window in the master bedroom and the custom oversize doors at front and back—set the personality of the house and do double duty by providing both ornament and amenity. If I were to make a rule to guide economical design, it would be, Keep it simple and trust in the power of a few strong moves.

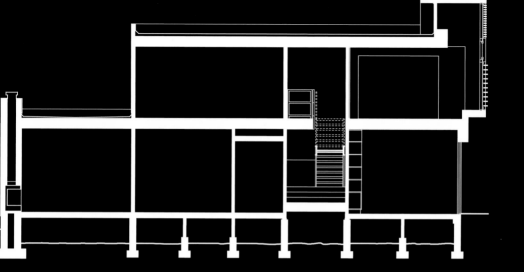

3.

Fit

As a rule,
communities are most comfortable with deference
as the approach to architectural legacy.
The expectation is that new buildings,
to fit with the old, should be contextual.

Some clients demand that architects
match a favored traditional style or local landmark,
and many architects are comfortable with this stipulation.
It is certainly easier to gain acceptance
with a proposition wrapped in historic ornament.
However, I am not sure that style buys the quality of life
that communities associate with the past.
It is easy to forget that much now hallowed historic building stock
lay vacant or underutilized for years.
It is likely that *lifestyle* rather than *style* is the key.
Making places comfortable for everyday living
is more about an economic and social infrastructure
than an ornamental approach to building design.

The case against contextualism
is founded on the idea of a different,
equally limiting authenticity.
This point of view maintains that the obligation of architecture
is not to fit in with the past
but to represent the culture and technology of the time—
whatever that culture and technology might be.
This stance offers an easy framework,
especially for those who are predisposed to contemporary design,
but it is also rigid and narrow.
Contextualism is blind to any aspects of context
that do not conform to romanticized norms;
authenticity presumes that the only relevant aspects
of culture and technology
are those that support discernable newness.

Adopting a *loose fit* mind-set might be more useful
for designing in established places.
It would allow for more thoughtful readings of context
and more flexible approaches to building new;
at the very least, it would make for a more tolerant debate.
The extreme positions might work well for Monticello
or the Pompidou Center,
but the communities where we have worked
are filled with nuances that are not always detected
by an overly sensitive contextualism or an insensitive authenticity.

American Craft Museum

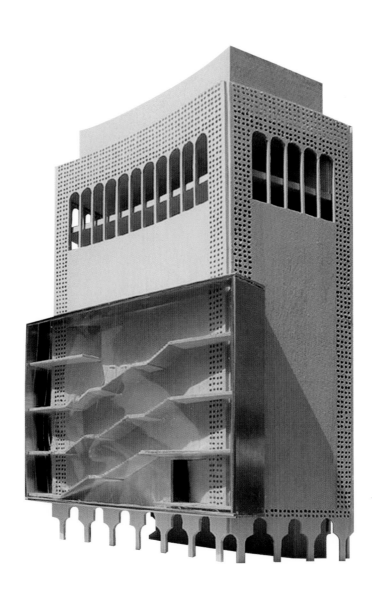

Well before the new millennium, the Gallery of Modern Art at 2 Columbus Circle, designed in the 1960s by Edward Durell Stone for collector Huntington Hartford, was considered neither people-friendly nor pretty. Even so, the building held a strong place in the cultural memory of New York City. It didn't seem right to abandon her just because she had aged poorly. So when we were included in a limited competition in 2002 to transform the vacant icon for the American Craft Museum (since renamed the Museum of Arts & Design), we tried to keep as much of it as possible. The project, resonating with a human condition rather than an abstract proposition, was strongly appealing: it featured a reclusive building, a populist program focusing on craft (not art), and the need for the most pragmatic of solutions.

Given the tight budget, analysis of practical concerns had to drive the design approach. The existing circulation was not code-compliant or efficient; we focused on how to lend conceptual backing to correcting these deficiencies. Because the floor plates were so tiny, any improvements in circulation came at the expense of exhibit space, so we slid the main museum stair outside the exterior wall of the building. In this location, the stair would not only release floor space but provide visitors with views over Central Park. The building's Venetian roots suggested the slumped-glass enclosure that modified this quintessential New York view into a blurry underwater panorama. From the street, people would see museum visitors moving up and down the stair, at long last suggesting a more sociable relationship between the building and the city. The load-bearing concrete-wall construction prohibited large span openings between the stair and the exhibit space; instead, small openings cut into the corners of each floor provided the link. Keeping the exterior concrete walls more or less intact made sense for other reasons: the approach provided light-controlled exhibit spaces and stayed true to Stone's interest in the strength and plasticity of concrete.

The next task was to identify a strategy to add upper-floor windows to the blank facades. The building was ornamented with perforated borders and a gridded marble field that had an uncanny resemblance to an incomplete needlework sampler— and that became the inspiration. It was a coincidence suited to the agenda and audience of a craft museum and also to our own curiosity about domestic crafts. With Andrea Keller, an architect and expert on anything woven, knitted, or threaded, we established a window ordering system that used architecture to acknowledge handicraft, creating a knitting pattern from the building overlay. We made samplers to test the idea. New windows denoted bobbles, LED lights indicated purl stitch, empty grids represented stockinette stitch, and diagonal aluminum bars signified cable stitch. It seemed fitting that a craft museum should have its own esoteric code, one that could be understood by knitters and other handworkers. Although we did not win the commission, it is still viscerally satisfying to think that a building might be knitted like a sock.

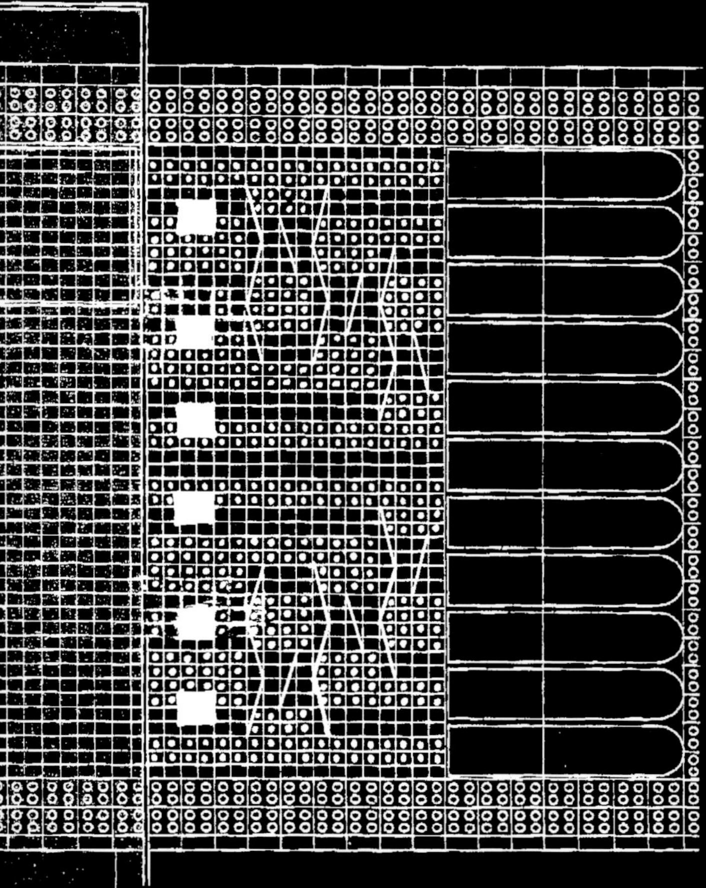

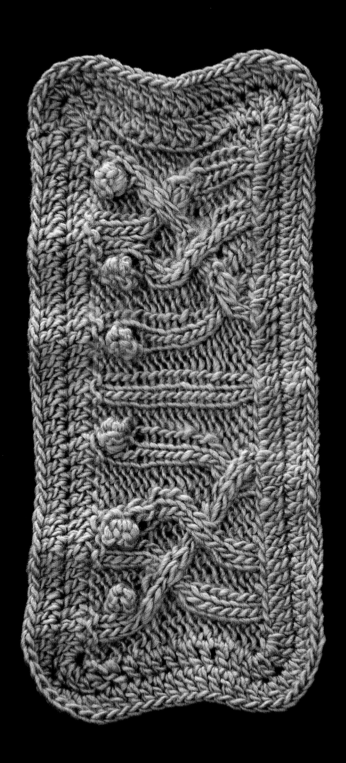

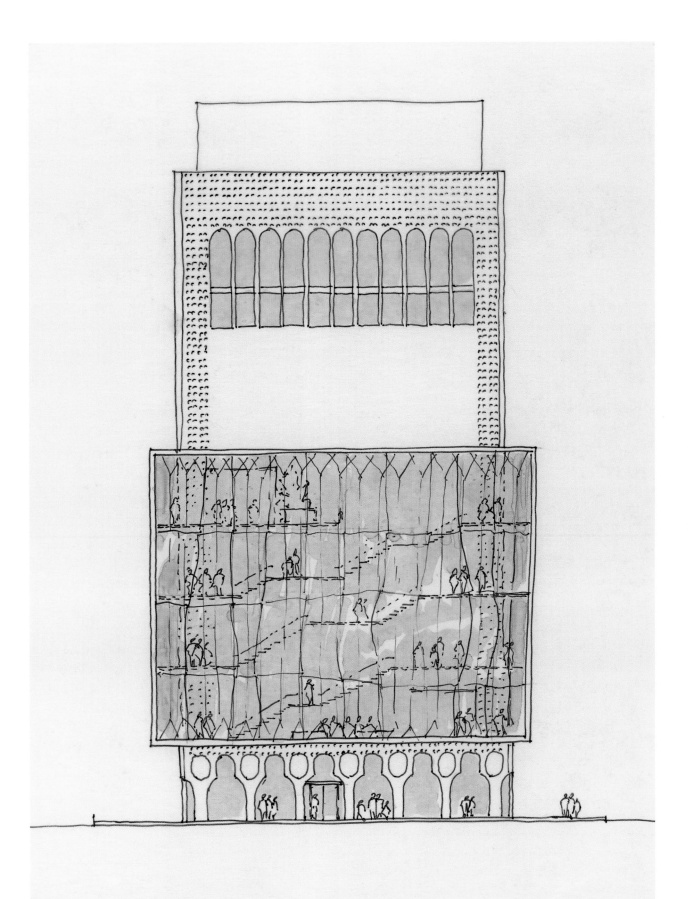

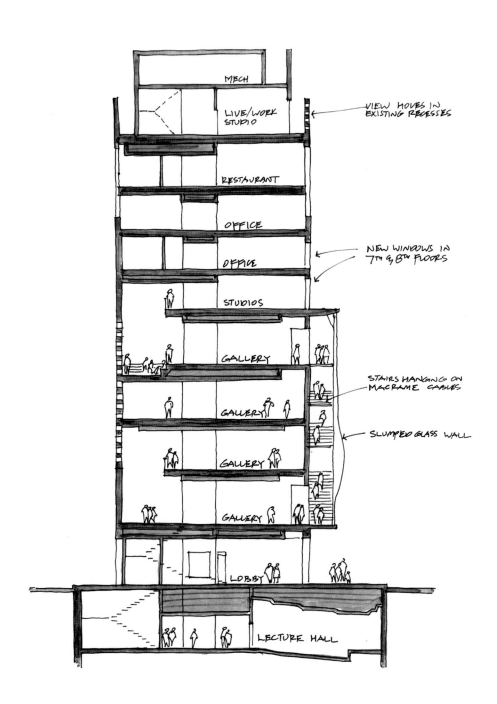

MECH

LIVE/WORK STUDIO

VIEW HOLES IN EXISTING RECESSES

RESTAURANT

OFFICE

OFFICE

NEW WINDOWS IN 7TH & 8TH FLOORS

STUDIOS

GALLERY

GALLERY

STAIRS HANGING ON MACRAME CABLES

GALLERY

SLUMPED GLASS WALL

GALLERY

LOBBY

LECTURE HALL

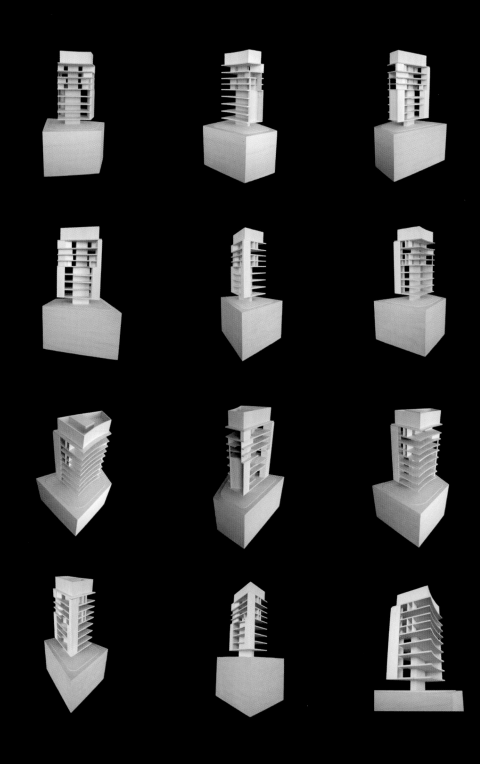

Farmers Market

The Los Angeles Farmers Market is a cultural icon. We were students when we first discovered it in 1980. The market broke all the rules of textbook urbanism—it was inward-looking and surrounded by cars—but it was wonderful. Inside were tree-canopied dining patios and narrow canvas-covered aisles lined with small stores. As we learned later, the market grew from informal beginnings in the 1930s into its picture-postcard heyday in the 1950s. By the 1980s, business had faded a little—but the attraction had not.

We started working on the market (owned by the Gilmore Company) soon after leaving school. Our early projects introduced us to its subtlety. We reconfigured gateways, remodeled dining patios, and designed new stalls. The charm of the market was partly to do with the sense of discovery and partly to do with the unpretentious setting that supported individual merchant's changing displays. While visitors romanticized the farmyard vernacular—though there wasn't all that much of it—it was really the ad hoc merchandising that was key to the atmosphere. Through this work, it became apparent to us that architects' architecture did not have all the answers to making sustainable social spaces. There was a lot to learn from vernacular settings.

In 1998, plans to build a regional shopping center—the Grove— to the east of the Farmers Market (on land owned by Gilmore) set in motion a complementary master plan for the market. The proposal centered on reviving and enhancing the historic property. Although the Grove and the Market were separate developments, synergy between the two, established in part by a strong pedestrian connection, was essential, as was retaining easy surface parking for market patrons. The ecology of the market operation, surface parking, pedestrian flow, and the needs of prospective retail tenants set the building disposition. The final plan added 120,000 square feet, organized in two large freestanding buildings and a collection of smaller infill pieces, to the 90,000-square-foot market.

Customers expected the romanticized market style, and we first investigated the obvious—replicating it. But it felt contrived to build so much "old" new. Moreover, modern retail, so grand in scale, would have appeared overblown clothed in the farmyard vernacular. It became apparent that any significant new buildings would need to be distinct from the original. This realization in turn suggested that the market's current nondescript exterior would need work to read as an identifiable destination within the new context.

So we grew the original market by adding matching infill buildings to activate the perimeter, renovating but not enlarging existing gateways, and even designing "home-made" market-style lounge chairs for the new north plaza, which was anchored by a relocated clock tower visible from the Grove. Remaining buildings were designed to be identifiably contemporary, though they draw loosely on market associations. The design approach to the market was not about stylistic etiquette but focused instead on how to use additions (big or small) to make comfortable transitions, backdrops, and thresholds to a historic but casual place.

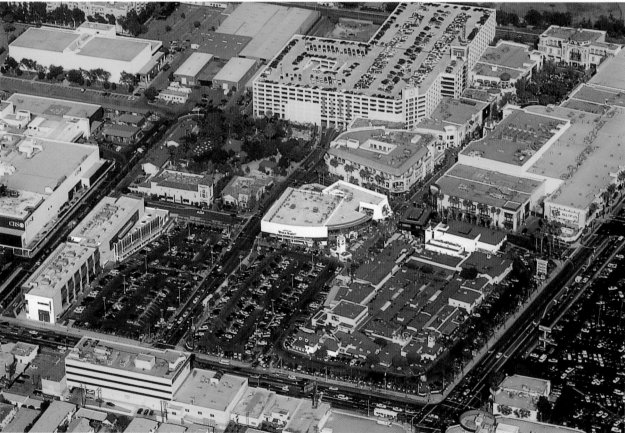

Big-box retail, stores; office space above

Relocated clock tower

Market operations

Historic Gilmore adobe house and garden

Gilmore Bank

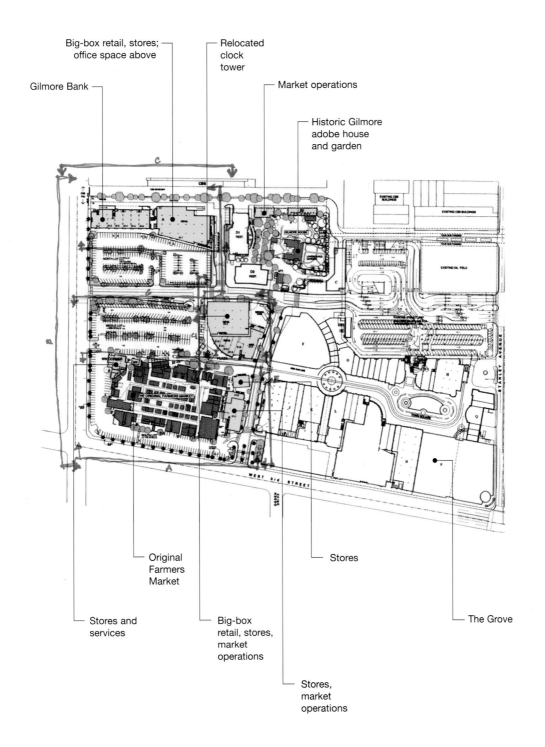

Original Farmers Market

Stores

Stores and services

Big-box retail, stores, market operations

The Grove

Stores, market operations

I'm here every morning.

Juanita Morgan, Farmers Market regular for twenty-five years

Avalon Hotel

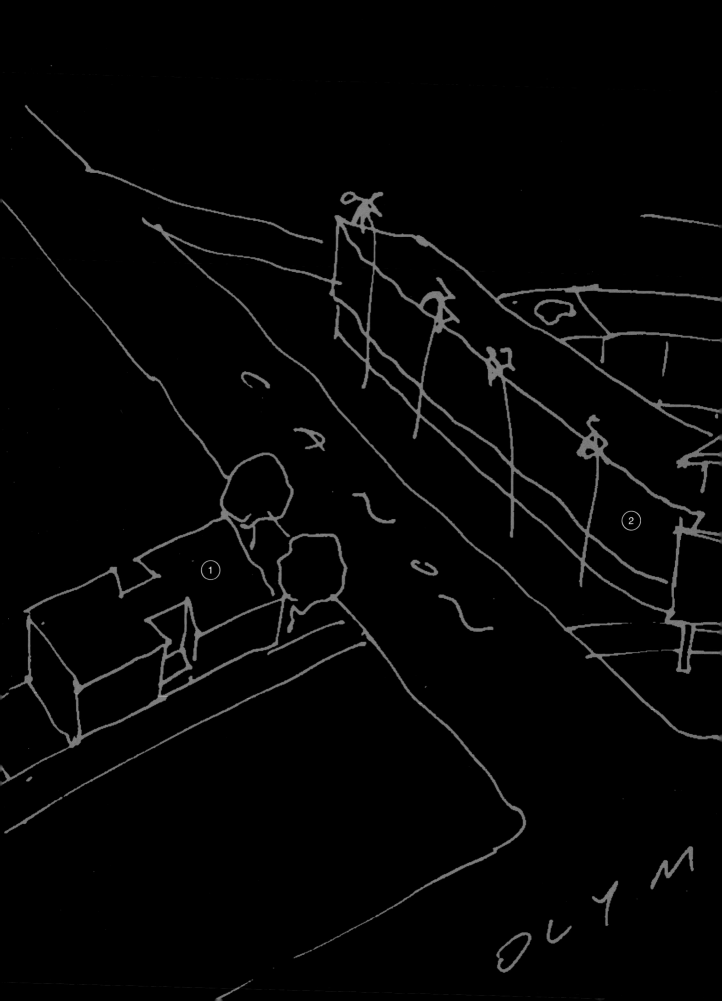

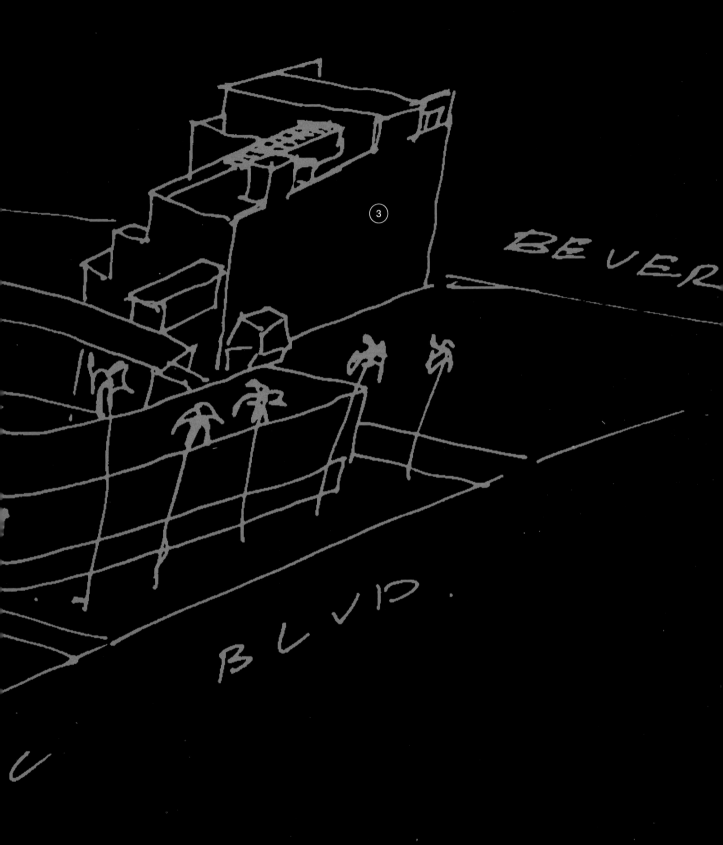

Building 1

Building 2

Building 3

The Avalon Hotel, at the corner of Olympic Boulevard and Canon Drive in Beverly Hills, looks like one building but in fact comprises three. The centerpiece, housing the main entrance and all public spaces, was built in 1948 on the corner site; over the next fifteen years, the hotel expanded to include two bland guest-room buildings nearby. The place had certainly slipped from the days when Marilyn Monroe slept there. The recently added "puffy-sleeve" barrel-vaulted awnings and elaborate French doors sat uncomfortably on the fading midcentury modern structure they so desperately sought to improve. By the late 1990s, all three buildings needed attention, but the piloti-supported main building needed it most.

It was around this time that midcentury modernism was beginning to recapture the public's affection—though no one much cared about the fate of the Beverly Carlton, as the Avalon was then known. When we first toured the building, we were surprised at how cramped the public spaces felt. From the outside, expressive oversized columns, which carried three levels of guest rooms, promised an open and generous ground floor that flowed lazily to the pool beyond, but this was not the case. The limited budget, which precluded anything more than minimal structural changes, in effect encouraged commitment to the existing design, and we set about both reviving and inventing its strengths. Our approach was more improv than researched. Research is useful to validate strategy, but observation and compositional analysis are key to understanding the essence of any design.

Obvious detritus, like the awnings and French doors, was the first to go; then color was used to bolster the underlying form. Original features were reinterpreted—the corner facade became a plaid billboard. We opened the skinny ground-floor interior into one long space with a floating check-in counter at one end. A new blue terrazzo floor, poured inside and out, emphasizes the connection between the pool area and the simplified interior. The elevator, too small to be code compliant, was removed, allowing, for the first time, a direct view from entry to courtyard. The new elevator sits in a folded, copper-clad tower at the edge of the courtyard. The side walls of the old elevator shaft were retained to support upper floors, while the cab space was replaced by a picture window. The expanded view highlights the existing backdrop of exterior cabanas, and the new trellis casts stripy 1950s movie shadows. Interior designer Kelly Wearstler selected furniture to complete the fantasy of glamorous poolside life.

Style trumps substance every time. (Was it Oscar Wilde who implied this?) In its own time, the architectural merit of the hotel played second fiddle to Marilyn Monroe's patronage, but now that midcentury modern architecture is fashionable again, even semivernacular examples like this have become celebrities. It is interesting that architects troubled by historic theming do not notice that such projects are just as historicist as the production design for *Gone with the Wind:* both play equally fast and loose with their ornament. The idea of a place like the Avalon is to fit the expectations of a particular lifestyle—to try it on. Make-believe is not a weakness; authenticity is not always the issue.

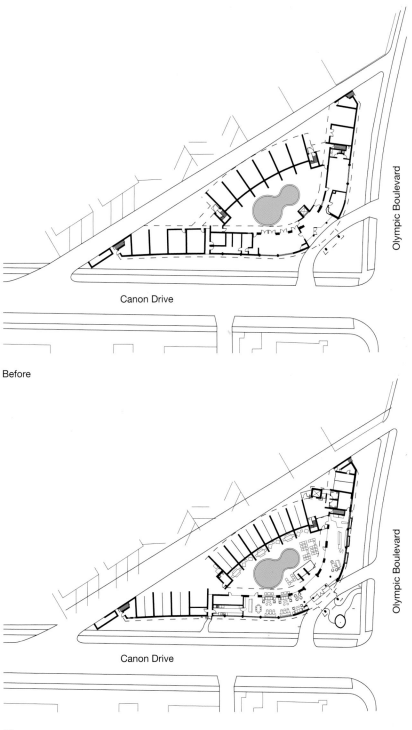

Before

After

Olympic Boulevard

Canon Drive

0 10 30 60 Feet

N

Children's Museum of Pittsburgh

Franz Kafka never visited the United States, but when he wrote about a mythic industrial city in *Amerika,* he must have been imagining Pittsburgh with its dramatic geography, stone-clad architecture, and soaring steel bridges. This past seemed almost overwhelming to us on the cloudy day in 2000 when we first visited the city as participants in an NEA-sponsored design competition to expand the Children's Museum of Pittsburgh. It is easy to forget the ingenuity that powered that legacy and focus only on the artifacts. Luckily, a good picture book can be as vivid as a Kafka novel. One favorite by Maira Kalman includes an old Chinese saying calling on parents to give their children roots and wings. It seemed like good advice for addressing the project's historic context.

The museum was housed in a 23,000-square-foot classical post office from the 1890s. The plan was to expand to 80,000 square feet, incorporating the adjacent Buhl Planetarium, built in 1939. The post office had a central domed hall that was naturally lit and cheerful, but the volume had been fragmented to accommodate museum programming. The windowless planetarium, on the other hand, was evocative but long vacant and a little grim. The museum envisioned an innovative and environmentally sustainable setting for children and their families with programs that would encourage kids to discover knowledge through hands-on activities. We followed the museum's lead, approaching the design as an armature for learning.

The two existing buildings are linked with a light-filled verandah. The glass and exposed-steel frame adds a different kind of architectural space to the carved volumes of the stone landmarks.

Ramps that connect the levels (old and new) exaggerate the sense of movement between both buildings and time periods. The historic interiors were honed, as budget and program permitted, to reveal the integrity of the original spaces. We cut a large opening in the east wall of the planetarium's grand lobby (somewhat controversially) and added giant illuminated spheres to supplement the light and animate the space.

To enclose new upper-level exhibit space, we proposed a folding polycarbonate translucent skin—a kind of Noguchi lantern/night-light. The lantern established a distinct presence on the domed skyline. After September 11, fundraising became more difficult. The *idea* of the lantern didn't fade, but the costs and risks of the folded assembly were considered too significant, and it was abandoned. At the same time, artist Ned Kahn, commissioned to design a water feature, was also rethinking his ideas. We pooled our budgets, hoping to buy the museum a bit more.

By this time, we had simplified the lantern into a straightforward glass and metal box wrapped on four sides with a flared, clip-on translucent sunshade. Some of Ned's wind pieces featured gridded fields of hinged metal plates that registered air currents. The idea had wings here, and we rethought the outer layer, cutting the translucent beaded-acrylic shade, conceptually and literally, into thousands of five-inch top-hinged flappers. The museum addition would be a lantern still, but a lantern wrapped in an "articulated cloud" (as Ned named the piece) that shades the glass and ripples in the wind. It was especially right for Pittsburgh, where the weather is a constant preoccupation.

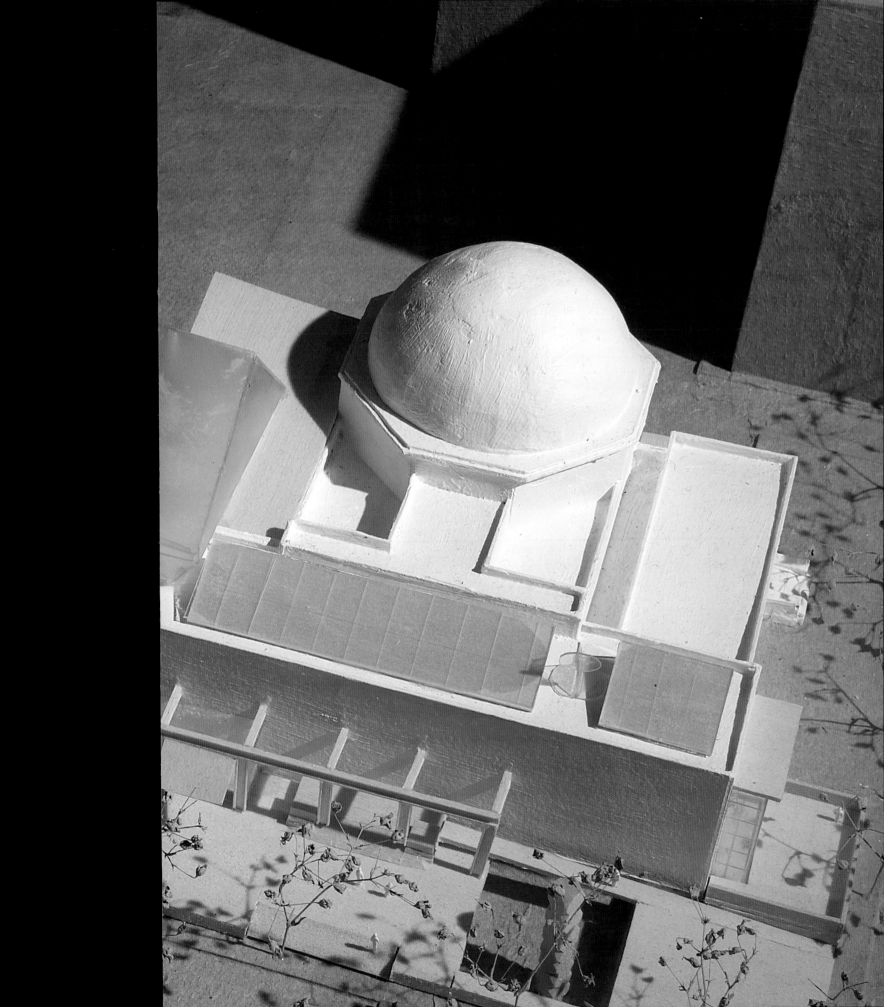

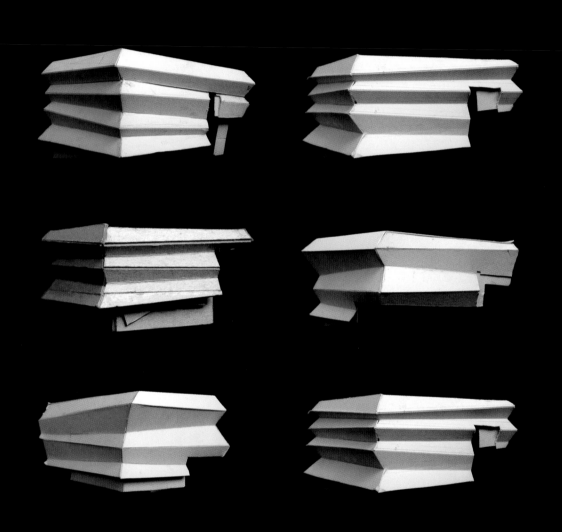

GLASS "TUNNEL CONNECTOR"

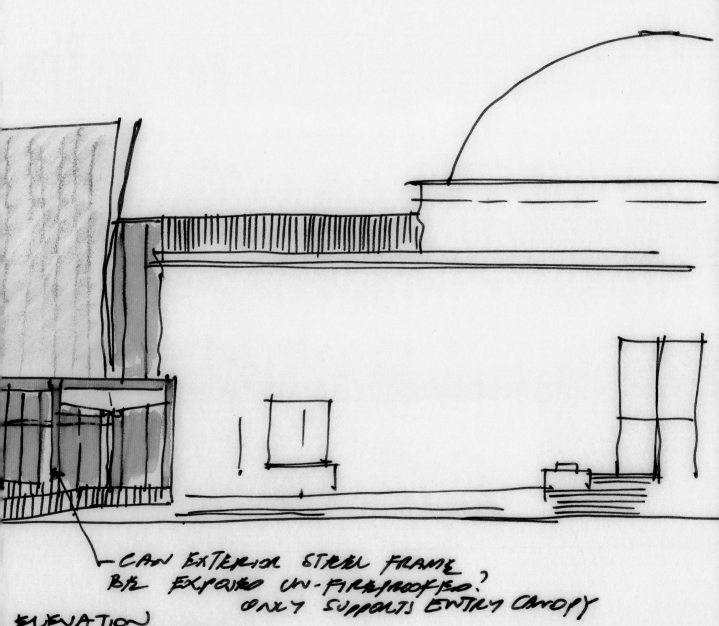

CAN EXTERIOR STEEL FRAME
B'2 EXPOSED UN-FIREPROOFED?
ONLY SUPPORTS ENTRY CANOPY

ELEVATION
KRS   12.16.02 .

A2/A3.1

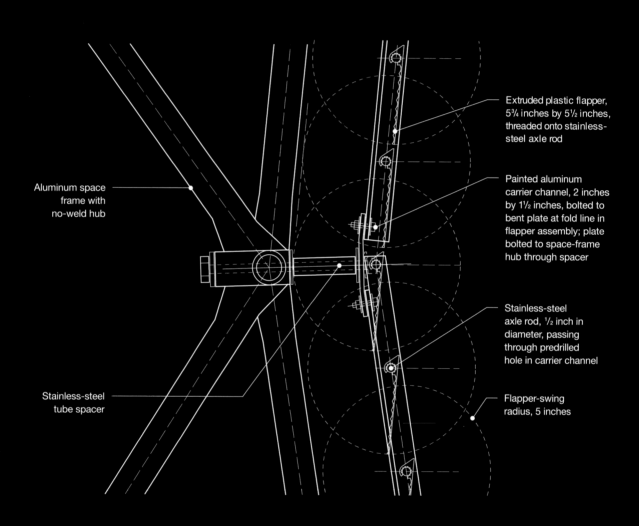

Aluminum space
frame with
no-weld hub

Stainless-steel
tube spacer

Extruded plastic flapper,
5¾ inches by 5½ inches,
threaded onto stainless-
steel axle rod

Painted aluminum
carrier channel, 2 inches
by 1½ inches, bolted to
bent plate at fold line in
flapper assembly; plate
bolted to space-frame
hub through spacer

Stainless-steel
axle rod, ½ inch in
diameter, passing
through predrilled
hole in carrier channel

Flapper-swing
radius, 5 inches

0   2   4   8   Inches

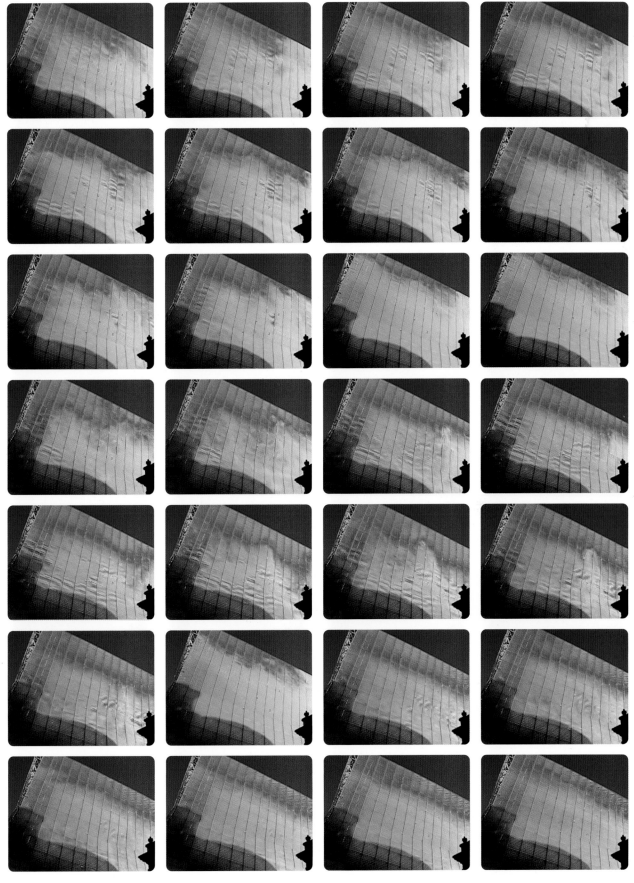

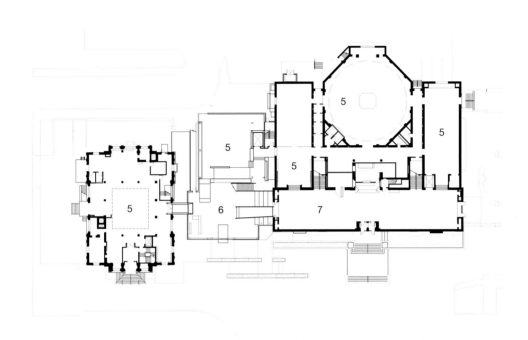

First Floor

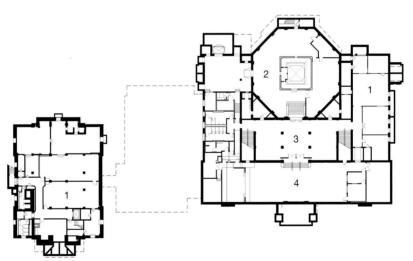

Basement

1 Classrooms	5 Exhibit	9 Head Start
2 Workshop/storage	6 Entry/verandah	10 Boardroom
3 Orientation	7 Lounge/cafeteria	
4 Theater	8 Administration	

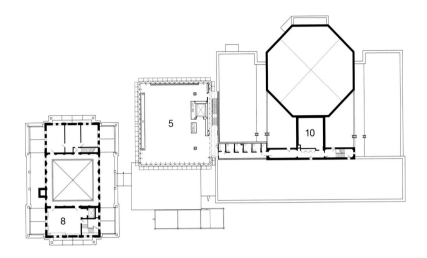

Third Floor

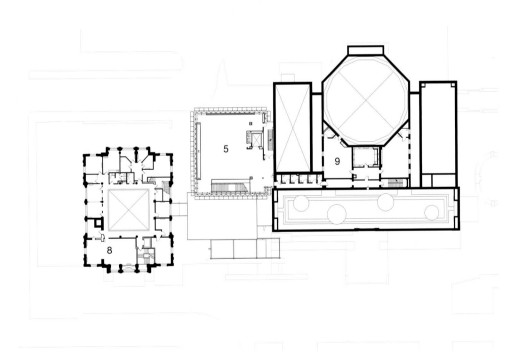

Second Floor

N

0 16 32   64   Feet

It's a great big playground in here.

Thorne Griffith, 9½

Acknowledgments

Without colleagues Jason Kerwin and Mohamed Sharif, who saw the
value in putting on paper the ideas we share, I would never have finished
this book. I am also indebted to Suzanne Hague and Meaghan McCall,
who bore the brunt of the image and research load.

Not everyone enjoys going to work, but I do. For that I must thank
Hank Koning, Brian Lane, current and past associates Jason Kerwin,
Ian Macduff, Oonagh Ryan, and Julio Zavolta, and the whole team
for their ingenuity, creativity, and dedication.

Bob Dinetz, the book's designer, burrowed into our heads to elucidate
a printed context for our ideas, and Andrea Monfried, our editor at
The Monacelli Press, has been a trusted critic of content and written word.

—J.E.

Biographies

Hank Koning, FAIA, FRAIA, received a bachelor of architecture degree
from the University of Melbourne in 1977 and a master of architecture
degree from the University of California, Los Angeles in 1981. Also in
1981, he cofounded Koning Eizenberg Architecture in Santa Monica.
Koning is a member of the U.S. Green Building Council and serves as
a planning commissioner for the city of Santa Monica.

Julie Eizenberg, AIA, earned a bachelor of architecture degree from
the University of Melbourne in 1977 and a master of architecture degree
from the University of California, Los Angeles in 1981. Later that year,
she cofounded Koning Eizenberg Architecture. Eizenberg teaches and
lectures throughout the United States and abroad.

Brian Lane received a bachelor of architecture degree from the California
Polytechnic State University, San Luis Obispo in 1986 and a master of
architecture degree from the University of Pennsylvania in 1990. Lane
worked for Koning Eizenberg from 1991 to 1993 and returned in 1998;
he became managing principal in 2003. Lane serves on the architectural
review board for Hollywood. He is an advocate for quality housing (both
affordable and market rate), advising on city ordinances that facilitate
housing production.

Project Credits

West Hollywood Community Center
West Hollywood, California, 1998–2001
Client: City of West Hollywood
Team: Julie Eizenberg, Hank Koning, Brian Lane, Naomi Neville,
Carole Chun, Jason Kerwin, Oonagh Ryan, Dason Whitsett, Julio Zavolta

***Masonry Variations* Exhibit**
National Building Museum, Washington, D.C., 2003–4
Client: International Masonry Institute
Exhibition Curator: Stanley Tigerman
Team: Julie Eizenberg, Hank Koning with Michael Menegazzi
(lead BAC craftworker), Roderick Villafranca, Shawn Bleet, Scott Walter

PS#1 Elementary School
Santa Monica, California, 1996–99
Client: PS#1 Elementary School
Team: Julie Eizenberg, Hank Koning, Tim Andreas, Carole Chun,
Jim Jackson, Kevin Tyrrell, Dason Whitsett

The Herb Alpert Educational Village
Santa Monica, California, 2001–8
Client: New Visions Foundation
Team: Julie Eizenberg, Hank Koning, Ian Macduff, James Kelly,
John Berry, Robert Fabijaniak, Shawn Bleet, Crystal Chan,
Sophie Dufresne, Suzanne Hague, Sarah Heller, Jason Kerwin,
Avi Laiser, Meaghan McCall, Paul Miller, Amy Pokawatana, Adam Polk,
Dan Sokolosky, Roderick Villafranca

Harold Way Apartments
Los Angeles, California, 2000–2003
Client: Hollywood Community Housing Corporation
Team: Julie Eizenberg, Hank Koning, Brian Lane, Roderick Villafranca,
Erin McLaughlin, Eleanor O'Neill

25th Street Studio
Santa Monica, California, 1998–99
Client: Hank Koning/Julie Eizenberg
Team: Julie Eizenberg, Hank Koning, Dason Whitsett,
Carole Chun, Julio Zavolta

West Street Community Center
New York, New York, 2002
Client: Visualization for the *New York Times*
Team: Julie Eizenberg, Hank Koning, Roderick Villafranca

The Standard Downtown L.A.
Los Angeles, California, 2000–2002
Client: Hotels AB
Team: Julie Eizenberg, Hank Koning, John Berry, Olivia Goff,
Eleanor O'Neill, Quito Banogon, Shawn Bleet, Amy Drezner,
Eric Elerath, Robert Fabijaniak, Avi Laiser, Erin McLaughlin,
Oonagh Ryan, Roderick Villafranca

Hancock Avenue Housing
West Hollywood, California, 1998–2007
Client: CIM Group, LLC
Team: Julie Eizenberg, Hank Koning, Brian Lane,
Jason Kerwin, Oonagh Ryan, Scott Walter, Crystal Chan,
Sophie Dufresne, Suzanne Hague, Paul Miller, Mohamed Sharif,
Dan Sokolosky, Julio Zavolta

11th Street House
Santa Monica, California, 1998–2001
Client: Jeffrey and Kimberly Shine
Team: Julie Eizenberg, Hank Koning, Fernando Bracer,
Oonagh Ryan, Dason Whitsett, Jason Kerwin, Naomi Neville

American Craft Museum (competition)

New York, New York, 2002

Client: American Craft Museum (now Museum of Arts & Design)

Team: Julie Eizenberg, Hank Koning, John Berry, Shawn Bleet, Robert Fabijaniak, James Kelly, Erin McLaughlin, Roderick Villafranca

Farmers Market

Los Angeles, California, 1998–2002

Client: A. F. Gilmore Company

Team: Julie Eizenberg, Hank Koning, Brian Lane, Julio Zavolta, Robert Kerr, Jason Kerwin, Avi Laiser, Erin McLaughlin, Eleanor O'Neill, Oonagh Ryan, Roderick Villafranca

Avalon Hotel

Beverly Hills, California, 1997–99

Client: Kor Group

Team: Julie Eizenberg, Hank Koning, Tim Andreas, Fernando Bracer, Carole Chun, Norah Edelstein, Jim Jackson, Dan Parks

Children's Museum of Pittsburgh

Pittsburgh, Pennsylvania, 2000–2004

Client: Children's Museum of Pittsburgh

Team: Julie Eizenberg, Hank Koning, Brian Lane, John Berry, Ian Macduff, Roderick Villafranca, Quito Banogon, Shawn Bleet, Amy Drezner, Robert Fabijaniak, James Kelly, Erin McLaughlin, Phillip Pare, Julio Zavolta

Photography Credits

Benny Chan/fotoworks: 66–67, 84–85, 92–93, 94, 95, 96, 102–3, 104, 105, 108–9, 114, 141, 142, 144, 145, 149, 152, 153, 154–55, 160–61, 164, 167, 168, 169, 170–71, 172–73, 174–75, 176–77, 178, 179, 242–43, 249, 250, 251, 252, 253, 254–55, 256–57, 324–25

Benny Chan/fotoworks; courtesy A. F. Gilmore Company: 280 (left column, second from top; right column, third from top), 283, 286–87, 288, 289, 290, 291, 294–95, 296, 297, 298–99

Grey Crawford: 307, 308, 309, 310–11, 312, 315, 316, 317

DigitalGlobe, Inc.: 45, 138, 188–89, 222–23

Bob Dinetz Design: 71

Courtesy A. F. Gilmore Company: 278–79, 280 (left column, first, third, and fourth from top; right column, first, second, and fourth from top)

Ned Kahn: 335

Koning Eizenberg Architecture: 46–47, 72, 73, 74–75, 76, 78, 79, 86, 89, 90–91, 106–7, 117, 118–19, 124, 126–27, 129, 130, 131, 132–33, 182, 183, 184, 186–87, 208, 209, 210, 211, 225, 226, 227, 228–29, 236–37, 238–39, 262, 263, 270, 272–73, 274–75, 304, 326, 327, 328–29, 330, 331, 344 (left column; right column, second and third from top)

Dennis McCarthy: 344 (right column, top)

Grant Mudford: 48, 50–51, 52, 53, 56, 57, 58, 59, 60–61, 62–63

Museum of Arts and Design Store: 268

Nagata Acoustics, Inc.: 122–23

Susan S. Peirce/www.canyonlights.com: 68

Sanborn Map Company: 198

Robert Schlatter: 54, 100, 150, 212, 292, 342

Angelica Solis: 112–13

Tim Street-Porter: 194, 199, 200–201, 202, 203, 204, 205, 206–7, 214, 215, 218–19

Albert Vecerka/Esto: 320–21, 336–37, 340–41, 344 (middle column; right column, bottom), 345, 346–47

Harry Zernike (courtesy National Building Museum): 80–81

First published in the United States of America in 2006 by
The Monacelli Press, Inc.
611 Broadway, New York, New York 10012

Copyright © 2006 by The Monacelli Press, Inc.

Library of Congress Cataloging-in-Publication Data
Eizenberg, Julie.
Architecture isn't just for special occasions :
Koning Eizenberg Architecture / [Julie Eizenberg].
p. cm.
ISBN 1-58093-170-7
1. Koning Eizenberg (Firm). 2. Architecture—United States—
20th century. 3. Architecture—United States—21st century.
I. Eizenberg, Julie. II. Title.
NA737.K68E47 2006
720.92'2—dc22   2006003513

Printed and bound in China

Designed by Bob Dinetz

www.kearch.com